Get Started *in*
LEATHER CRAFTING

Step-by-Step Techniques & Tips *for* Crafting Success

TONY LAIER, KAY LAIER

DESIGN ORIGINALS
an Imprint of Fox Chapel Publishing
www.d-originals.com

WELCOME TO LEATHER CRAFTING!

Historic, everlasting, classic, trending, creative, fun, a craft for all ages — these all describe leather crafting. It has been called the "universal craft" because it is shared with each generation around the world through hands-on teaching, demonstrations, experience, and exploration. We hope you will have fun and benefit from the basic techniques and tips shown in this book.

Tony & Kay

Tony Laier has over 40 years of experience in the leather industry: as Director of Research and Development for Silver Creek Leather Company and Tandy Leather Company, as leather artist, designer, writer, teacher, market manager and in direct sales. He is a musician, Native American hobbyist, and a Vietnam veteran. Tony received the 1999 Al Stohlman Award for Achievement in Leather Craft and now serves on the Board of Trustees for the Al and Ann Stohlman Award Foundation. He also is the master tooler for Steel Strike Leather Products, Inc., a high-end leather furniture company in Buena Vista, CO, where he currently lives and works with his wife, **Kay**. She, too, has over 40 years in the leather art and advertising profession at Silver Creek Leather Company, Tandy Leather Company, and Tandycrafts National Advertising. Together, they have co-authored this book to share their years of accumulated knowledge with leather crafters of all ages and levels of experience.

ISBN 978-1-4972-0346-4

© 2017 by Tony and Kay Laier and New Design Originals Corporation, *www.d-originals.com*, an imprint of Fox Chapel Publishing, 800-457-9112, 903 Square Street, Mount Joy, PA 17552.

We are always looking for talented authors. To submit an idea, please send a brief inquiry to acquisitions@foxchapelpublishing.com.

Printed in Singapore
Sixth printing

CONTENTS

ABOUT LEATHER: THE BASICS

For centuries, animal skins have been tanned to prepare them for use as garments, accessories, saddles, tack, utility items, and bindings. The animals that leather comes from can be grouped in two categories.

Domestic Animals: These are cows, pigs, and sheep, mostly by-products of the food industry.

Wild or Game Animals: Some are raised commercially, but most are taken in the wild. They include deer, elk, moose, bison, kangaroo, and some exotic animals like frogs, lizards, birds, and snakes.

LEATHER TANNING PROCESSES

There are many different tanning processes. Most common today are the vegetable-tanning and chrome-tanning processes.

1. Vegetable-Tanned (Veg-Tan) Leather

Hides are either suspended in pits or immersed in a large rotating drum in a tanning solution made by extracting the natural tannins or various trees and their bark. This produces leather suitable for hand tooling or stamping, machine embossing, molding, dyeing, and finishing.

2. Chrome-Tanned Leathers

This tannage uses chromium salts and takes much less time to process than veg-tan leather. It produces soft finished and suede leathers used for garments, footwear, upholstery, and more.

LATIGO LEATHER

Latigo is cowhide that is combination tanned—both chrome- and veg-tanned. Normally mid to heavy weights, this leather is strong and durable, suitable for belts, straps, lace, footwear, horse tack, and outdoor gear.

SUEDES

Ideal for craft and fashion accessories, lace, belts, and garments. Most, but not all, garment suede is chrome tanned. Suedes have been chrome tanned, sanded, and brushed on one or both sides for a soft, textured surface. One side usually has a finer texture. Suedes are pre-dyed, ready to cut, punch, and assemble into any size project. They are available in precut small pieces or full skins and sides. Sueded animal skins are made from cowhide splits, goat, pigskin, and deerskin.

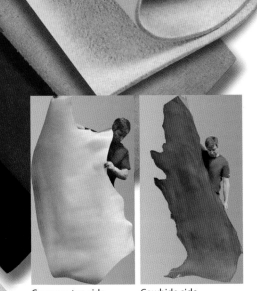

Cow veg-tan side   Cowhide side

Latigo leather

Suede is also used for lace and is available in precut strips and rectangular pieces.

Leather is measured by weight (1 oz. weight = ¹⁄₆₄" thickness). Here's a guide to help you select leather for your projects.

Weight, Thickness, and Common Uses

▬	2 to 3 oz.	(¹⁄₃₂" to ³⁄₆₄")	(.8 mm to 1.2 mm)	For molding, appliqués, linings, embossing, and jewelry
▬	3 to 4 oz.	(³⁄₆₄" to ¹⁄₁₆")	(1.2 mm to 1.6 mm)	For embossing, clutches, wallets, linings, and small kits
▬	4 to 5 oz.	(¹⁄₁₆" to ⁵⁄₆₄")	(1.6 mm to 2.0 mm)	For handbags, conceal carry holsters, wristbands, and appliqués
▬	5 to 6 oz.	(⁵⁄₆₄" to ³⁄₃₂")	(2.0 mm to 2.4 mm)	For lightweight cases, satchels, holsters, and journal covers
▬	6 to 7 oz.	(³⁄₃₂" to ⁷⁄₆₄")	(2.4 mm to 2.8 mm)	For handbags, cases, holsters, belts, and straps
▬	7 to 8 oz.	(⁷⁄₆₄" to ¹⁄₈")	(2.8 mm to 3.2 mm)	For belts, sheaths, holsters, handles, and straps
▬	8 + above	(¹⁄₈" + above)	(3.2 mm and above)	For holsters, belts, saddles and tack, straps, shoe soles, and armor

PREFINISHED LEATHERS

These leathers are available to the crafter in full hides, skins, sides, precut pieces, and lace, ready to cut to size for your project assembly. No dyeing or finishing is necessary. The most common sources are cow, calf, goat, pig, and deer.

Deerskins and deertan kidskins are soft, pliable, and available in precut pieces or full skins. Pre-dyed in a variety of colors, this leather is considered to be lightweight. The top side has a fine, pebbled grain, while the back is sueded. It can be cut with leather shears, a rotary cutter, or a die-cutting machine, and is used for garments, upholstery, lace, fringe, and more.

Decorative Prefinished Trim Leathers: These precut pieces come in a variety of embossed or stamped designs, textures, finishes, colors, and some come with hair on. They are perfect for craft projects and creative techniques.

PRE-EMBOSSED LEATHERS

These very popular and affordable leathers are created when a permanent texture is pressed into a skin. This can give the leather (normally cowhide) the look and feel of an embellished grain, tooled design, or particular exotic animal such as crocodile or ostrich. Embossed leather is available with or without color and a finish. They are ideal for fashion accessories, and craft and home décor projects.

HAIR-ON LEATHER

These skins have been tanned but not de-haired. Hair-on leathers are most often used as craft and home decor accents. Full hides, skins, and precut pieces are available in cow, calf, rabbit, sheep, bison, and more.

REMNANTS

Remnants are normally pieces of leather left over from the manufacturing process. These may come from factories producing shoes, furniture, bags, cases, or other leather goods. Some of the leathers included are cowhide, deerskin, latigo, prefinished leathers, and suedes.

Deerskin

Goat Full Skin

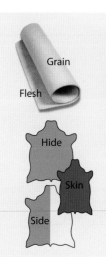

HERE ARE SOME HELPFUL TERMS

Grain Side: The top, smooth, outer side of a piece of leather.

Flesh Side: The underside or rough side of a piece of leather.

Hide: The whole pelt of a large animal.

Skin: The whole pelt of a small animal.

Side: Half of a hide or skin.

Grain

Flesh

Hide

Skin

Side

Back

Belly

Single Shoulder

Double Shoulder

Back: A side with the belly section removed. The back is firmer than the belly.

Belly: The lower part of a side. The belly has more stretch than the back.

Single Shoulder: The "single" shoulder area of a side.

Double Shoulder: The "double" shoulder area of a full hide.

For more terminology, see the Glossary on pages 46–47.

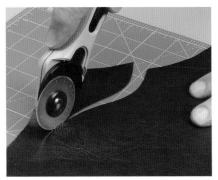

Rotary cutter

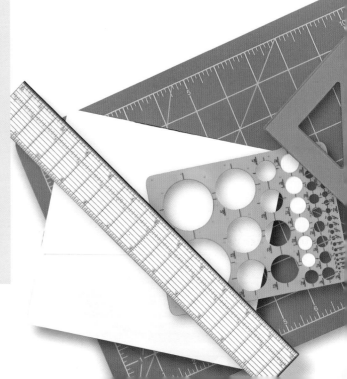

Self-healing cutting mat

TOOLS FOR CUTTING LEATHER

ROTARY CUTTER
This popular tool is used for cutting straight and slightly curved cuts.
- Ideal for cutting soft, stretchy leathers.
- Use a straight edge for easier cutting.
- Replace the blade when it's dull.

CRAFT AND BOX KNIVES
These knives are a must for leather craft projects.
- Use a plastic or metal straight edge for easier cutting.
- Turn the leather so the cut parts are closest to you.
- Keep the blades sharp by stropping. See page 13 for how to make a strop and use it, or have replacement blades available.

LEATHER SCISSORS AND SNIPS
Leather scissors are used for light to medium weights of leather, lace, and thread.
Leather snips are best for lightweight leather, lace, and thread.

SELF-HEALING CUTTING MAT
Use to ease cutting and protect your work surface. The self-healing feature prevents your knife from slipping into previous cut lines, plus the mat will last longer.

POLYETHYLENE CUTTING BOARD
Protects your work surface from cutting, punching holes, and tooling.

STRAIGHT EDGES, SQUARES, TEMPLATES
Handy tools to make cutting easier.

TIPS: CUTTING DIFFERENT LEATHERS

Cutting Veg-Tan, Prefinished, and Suedes: Place leather right side up on the mat. Be sure your knife is sharp (stropped). Suede particles will form on the cut lines, so use a lint roller to remove them.

Cutting Hair-on Leather: Cut on the backside, just through the leather. Then pull pieces apart, carefully separating the hair. Pull along the edges to remove loose hairs.

Cutting Thick Leather: Try to cut through with the first cut. If you have to go back, carefully line up the blade in the previous cut groove and repeat the cut.

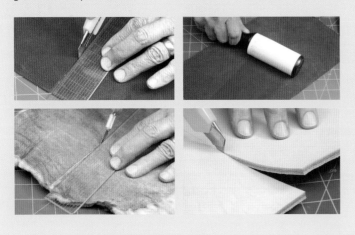

PREPARING LEATHER FOR TOOLING

Before you stamp or carve designs in leather, here are some basic preparation suggestions and steps to ensure more successful tooling.

MOUNTING LEATHER

To keep your leather from stretching during tooling, mount the leather on a sturdy surface, such as an illustration board (firm cardboard, but not corrugated). Some toolers use plexiglass. This is important when tooling on light- to medium-weight leathers. It may not be necessary for very small projects.

To mount:

- Apply a light coat of rubber cement to the board's surface with a stiff brush, plastic spreader, or piece of cardboard with a straight cut edge.
- When the glue loses its shine, it's time to place the leather.
- Press the leather down. You can use a brayer (roller).

TIP: When your tooling is completed and dry on the board, remove it from the leather by bending the board. Do not bend the leather. If using plexiglass, carefully use a metal or plastic kitchen spatula to release the leather.

CASING (DAMPENING) LEATHER

Veg-tan leather must be "cased" or dampened with clean water before it can be tooled.

- Apply water to the surface using a sponge.
- Let it sit for a few minutes until the water is absorbed. Then apply a second coat of water.
- When the leather returns to its natural color and is "cool" to the touch, it is ready to tool.
- Unfinished cased leather marks easily. Remove your rings, watches, and bracelets.

PREPARING A TOOLING PATTERN

Select a pattern from digital files, a pattern book, or draw your own. Here are some basic steps to help you.

Vellum: Draw or trace your pattern onto tracing paper or vellum, a semitransparent, sturdy tracing paper, using a pencil (so if you need to erase a line, you can).

Use a copier: Vellum is copier friendly, so make it easy on yourself and use it for making fast, multiple copies.

Use a stylus: Use the stylus end of a modeling tool to transfer your pattern to the cased leather. Check before removing the vellum pattern to be sure lines were not missed.

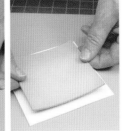

Mounting leather

Brayer

TIP: When working with unfinished leather, be sure that your hands and work space are clean! Dirt, grease, food, and sweat can easily stain the leather and ruin your project.

Casing (dampening) leather

TIP: If you need to stop during tooling, place the leather in a plastic bag to keep it from drying out. Close the bag and place a heavy book on top to keep the leather flat. When you're ready to start again, lightly re-case the entire surface, especially heavy around edges, using a sponge or spray bottle.

Transfer the pattern to cased leather.

Trace the pattern.

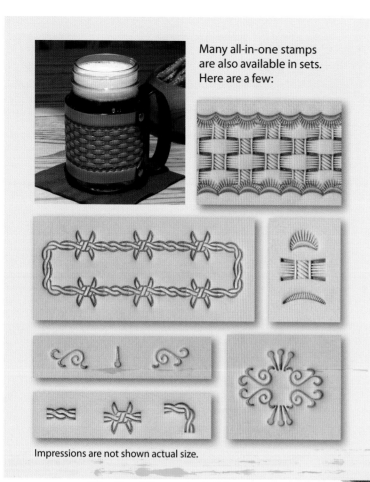

Many all-in-one stamps are also available in sets. Here are a few:

Impressions are not shown actual size.

THE BASICS OF STAMPING

Stamping designs, borders, sayings, names, initials, and more on veg-tan leather is fun and a great way to personalize your projects.

STAMPS ARE OFFERED IN TWO CONFIGURATIONS

1. Stamp Heads with a Separate Handle
- These stamp heads are usually sold in sets.
- Each set will include one handle that fits and locks into the stamp heads.
- Extra handles are also sold individually.

2. Full Stamps with Handles Included
- These stamps are grouped in "categories" (see next page). Within each category, there are multiple sizes, face designs, and textures.
- There are hundreds of different stamp designs.

TIP: To help identify and line up impressions, stamp heads normally have a mark (a dot, initial, or number) on the back.

Alignment dot

HEAD AND HANDLE SETS

Stamp heads come in sets, along with a separate handle. They include alphabets, numbers, sayings, designs, bugs, tracks, shapes, and more. Just a few of the options are shown here.

Stamps and impressions are not shown actual size.

BASIC CATEGORY GROUPS OF INDIVIDUAL STAMPS

There are many different face designs, textures, and sizes available in each category of stamps.
Impressions shown here are actual size.

Backgrounders (Matting)
Available in different sizes and textures.

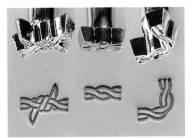

Barb Wire
Link the stamp sections together to create the impression of continuous wire.

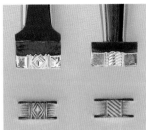

Basketweave
Many designs are available. See pages 11–12 for techniques.

Bevelers
Add depth by pushing leather back around your design.

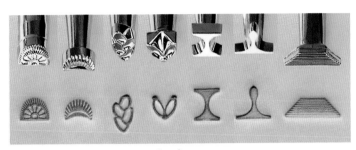

Borders
There are many designs, shapes, and sizes available for creating designs, borders, and background patterns by using these stamps alone or with other stamps.

Camouflages
"Cams"
Use to texture certain areas of a design and for borders.

Figure Carving
Created for pictorial/figure carving, and also used for borders and designs.

Flower Centers
Available in a variety of styles, sizes, and shapes.

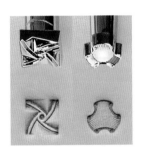

Geometrics
Use alone or in a joined series to create uniform designs in large areas.

Mulesfoot
Stamped alone or in a series at the end of a carved line or stop.

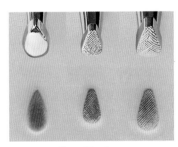

Pear Shaders
Use to shade areas of a design. Available with a smooth, lined, or checkered face.

Seeders
Use for flower seeds, and design and border elements.

Special
Many shapes, designs, and sizes, some lefts and rights are available.

Stops
Designed to "stop" a line. Also makes creative designs.

Veiners
Use to make veins in leaves plus to create borders and designs.

HOW TO USE STAMPS WITH SEPARATE HEADS OR FULL STAMPS

First, set up your work space with good lighting on a sturdy work table, and a chair so you can see over your work. Then assemble these supplies:

- Poly board, or hard stamping surface such as marble or granite slab
- Mallet or maul
- Bowl of water and sponge
- Selected stamps for designs

TIP: Let the leather dry completely, then add color and a protective finish (see pages 25–27).

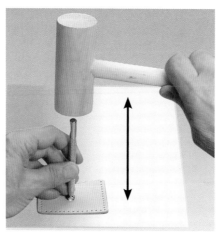

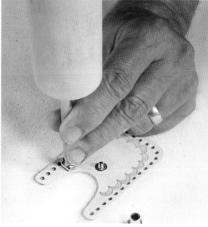

1. Before you stamp veg-tan leather, it must be dampened (cased) with water and a sponge. This softens the surface so impressions will show. When leather returns to its original color and is cool to the touch, it is ready to stamp.

2. Hold stamp firmly, straight up and down, and hit with a mallet or maul, also held straight up and down.

3. Check to see if the impression is deep enough. Hit again if necessary.

PATTERN IDEAS AND TECHNIQUES USING STAMPS AND A SWIVEL KNIFE

Plan the spacing of your impressions on a scrap piece of leather before working on your project leather. Corners are a good place to take up any extra space. Add different stamps to create accented corners.

Used with swivel knife borders (also see page 18)

TIP: Use rawhide, polyethylene, nylon, or wood mallets or mauls on stamping and punching tools; never use a metal hammer, which will damage the tools.

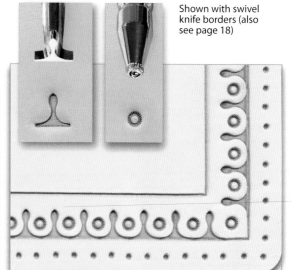

Shown with swivel knife borders (also see page 18)

Figure carving stamp used as a border tool

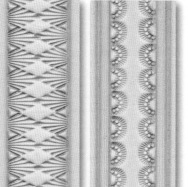

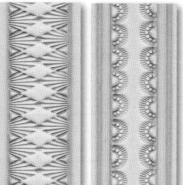

HOW TO STAMP A HEART DESIGN WITH AN HOUR-GLASS BORDER STAMP

1. Scribe a very light guideline through the center of the space to be stamped.
2. Stamp the first impression at an angle, aligning the tips of the tool on the guideline.
3. Carefully build the second row off the first row to form hearts.
4. Add more guidelines (if needed) to help keep the stamping straight.

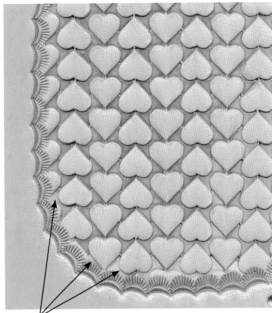

To allow space for a different border stamp to be added around the heart pattern, tilt the stamp to create partial impressions at a desired distance from the edge. Practice on scrap leather.

HOW TO STAMP AN ARROW BASKETWEAVE PATTERN

1. Using a stylus or swivel knife, outline (scribe a guideline A) around the space to be stamped.
2. Lightly press (ghost) the stamp below guideline A to mark the ends.
3. Scribe #2 light guideline B up from the center of the ghost impression.
4. Align the tips of the tool on the ghost impression and guideline B. Stamp #1 impression firmly using a mallet or maul.
5. Continue on both sides of the guideline. Impressions will form triangles.

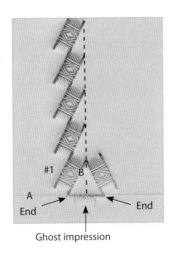

#1
B
A
End   End
Ghost impression

Continue

Add a decorative border stamp

HOW TO STAMP A BASKETWEAVE DESIGN

There a two basic ways to stamp basketweave designs: "diagonally" across your project (shown in the photos above) and "straight" through the center or along the edges of your project.

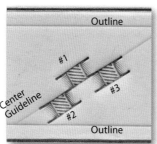

"Diagonal"

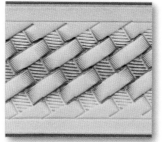

Partial impressions

Add a border stamp

1. Outline the space to be stamped with either a scribed line using a stylus or a cut line using a swivel knife.
2. Scribe a light guideline diagonally through the center of the space to be stamped.
3. Stamp the #1 impression on top of the guideline.
4. Stamp #2 and #3 below the guideline, overlapping the edges of the #1 impression.

5. Continue stamping, filling the space.
6. Tilt the tool to create partial impressions next to the edge of the space.
7. Add a decorative border with a border stamp or other stamps. Follow these same steps for a "straight" basketweave design.

TIPS:

When stamping around a curved edge, plan and practice the stamp design on scrap leather first.

Lightly scribe a guideline with a wing divider.

Be sure your stamps will "bend" around the edge.

For more depth, scribed guidelines can be cut and beveled before adding the border stamps.

TIP: By combining stamps, thousands of designs are possible. And by using the swivel knife (shown on pages 13–18), the number of possible designs is endless.

BORDER DESIGNS AND MORE

THE "CARVING" SWIVEL KNIFE

The swivel knife is "The Tool" for leather carvers. Its swivel action allows for smooth control while creating traditional floral carvings, swirling designs, monograms, flowing scrolls, and even hair on a bison.

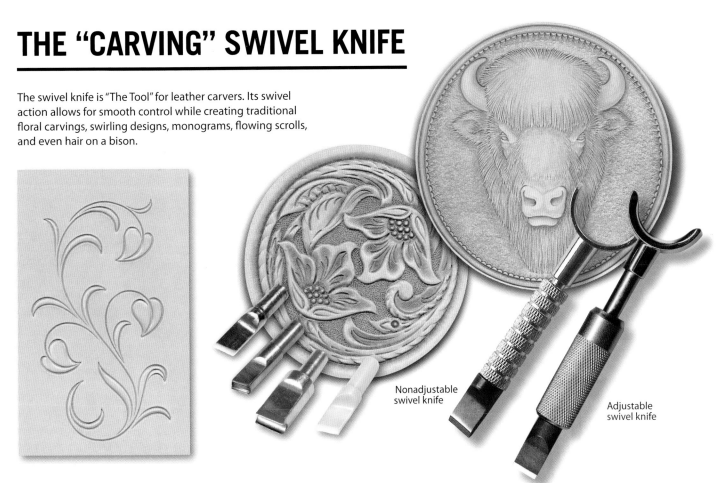

Nonadjustable swivel knife

Adjustable swivel knife

ABOUT THE SWIVEL KNIFE

Swivel knives come in many sizes and different styles. It is important to select the style and size that fits your hand and is comfortable to use.

While a straight blade is most commonly supplied with a new swivel knife, there are other options available, such as angle, hair, bead, and ceramic blades, and more.

Experiment with knives and blades to find one that works best for you.

STROP YOUR SWIVEL KNIFE

In order to carve leather, your swivel knife blade needs to be kept sharp (polished). If your blade is dull, your work will suffer and so will your hand. Most blades are pre-sharpened and only need to be stropped to keep them sharp.

How to Make a Sharpening/Polishing Strop:
1. Rub white polishing rouge on a piece of stiff cardboard.
2. Position the blade at an angle, resting the beveled edge flat on the strop.
3. Press and pull the blade toward you several times.
4. Strop both sides of blade.

THE PROPER WAY TO HOLD AND USE A SWIVEL KNIFE

- Hold the swivel knife straight up and down, tilted slightly forward while pulling (not pushing) toward you.
- Turn the leather for easier strokes.

The secret is practice! Before starting your project, practice on scrap leather to get a feel of the knife. Do the stroke exercises shown here to learn control.

TIP: There are different colors of polishing rouge. White is the cleanest and is preferred when working with leather.

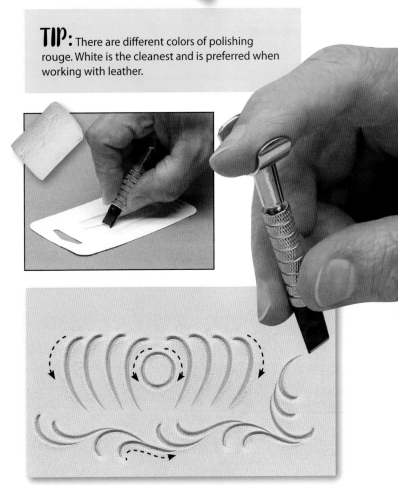

See pages 25–27 for coloring and finishing techniques.

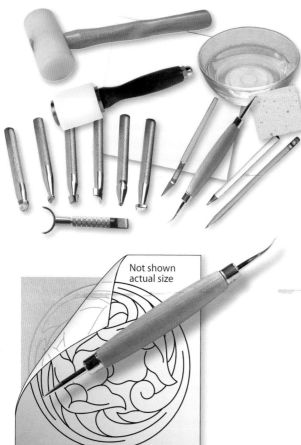

Not shown actual size

BASICS OF TRADITIONAL FLORAL CARVING

"Carving" leather refers to using a swivel knife to carve (cut) the surface of veg-tan leather. Other stamps are then used to create texture and dimension.

SET UP YOUR WORK SPACE
Assemble these general supplies and tools:
- Cutting mat
- Craft knife, scissors
- Poly board
- Mallet or maul
- Stylus (modeling tool)
- Pencil or pen
- Tracing vellum for pattern
- Bowl of water
- Sponge
- Swivel knife and blade
- Strop (cardboard strop and polishing rouge)
- Basic stamping tools
- Hard tooling surface (granite, marble, etc.)
- Natural light and lamps
- Sturdy work table and chair

STEP 1: PREPARE LEATHER, TRACE AND TRANSFER THE PATTERN TO LEATHER
Veg-tan leather must be dampened (cased) with water before it can be tooled. Apply water to the smooth (grain) side with a sponge. Leather is ready to carve when it starts to return to its natural color and is cool to the touch. Cased leather marks easily, so remove rings, bracelets, etc.

Use a pencil or ballpoint pen to draw or trace a pattern onto vellum. Use a stylus to transfer a pattern from vellum to cased leather. Check for missed lines before removing the vellum.

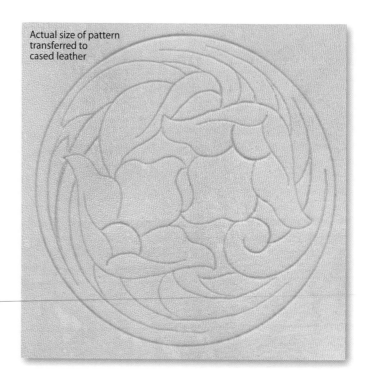

Actual size of pattern transferred to cased leather

TIP: Do a test tooling of your pattern to be sure the design corresponds with the size of your tools.

TIP: Use a plastic, ceramic, or glass bowl for water. Metal could create mineral deposits that will oxidize, creating dark spots on leather. To remove these spots, wipe leather with concentrated lemon juice. Then neutralize with water.

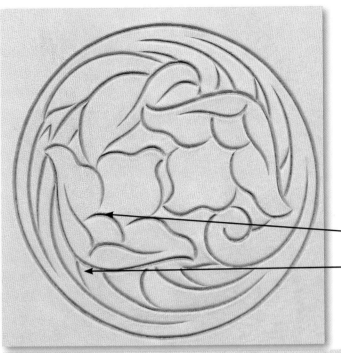

STEP 2: SWIVEL KNIFE

The depth of the cuts should be one-half the thickness of the leather. On thicker leathers, such as belt weight or saddle skirting, cut as deep as possible without distorting the lines.

There are many different blades available. Experiment with several until you find one you are comfortable using, or have different ones for different projects.

TIPS: Be sure your swivel knife blade is sharp and polished (see page 13).

You can cut the line for the center of a flower, or let the seed stamp (Step 17) create the outline.

Stop before getting to another cut line. This will prevent overcuts.

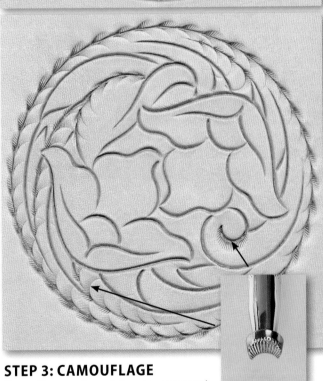

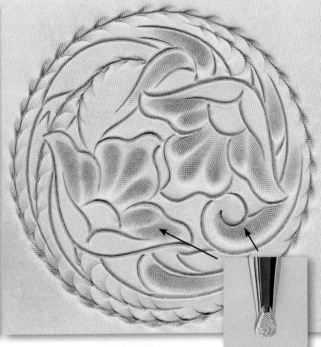

STEP 3: CAMOUFLAGE

Camouflages or "cams" disguise or conceal a line or edge. They can also be used for border designs and shapes.

STEP 4: PEAR SHADER

The pear shader is shaped like a pear. It is used to "shade" areas by adding depth and interest to a shape or design.

TIP: Create different effects by tilting, overlapping, and making pressure adjustments.

Tilt the tool for partial impressions.

Adjust pressure to create a dark to light effect.

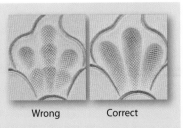

TIP: Overlap the impressions, and stamp with heavy to light pressure, creating a faded look. See page 16 for the "Walking the Tool" technique.

Wrong   Correct

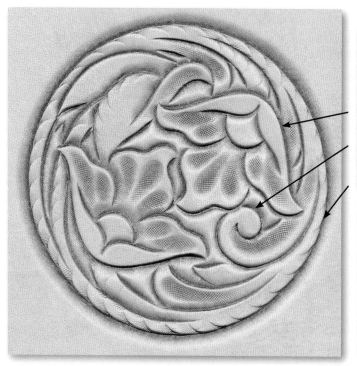

STEP 5: BEVELER

Bevelers add depth to your tooling. Beveling is done on one side or both sides of a swivel knife cut line. Decide where you want the leather beveled (pressed in) for the effect you want. Tip the edge of the tool that goes into the cut line. See below for the correct usage.

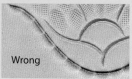

Into cut line

TIP: Practice beveling on scrap leather. See the Tip below for the "Walking the Tool" Technique.

Correct   Wrong

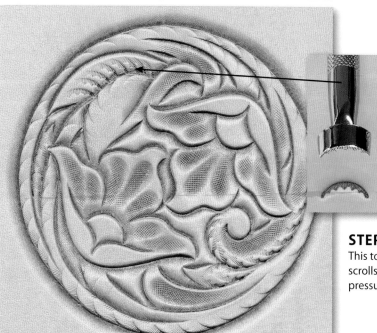

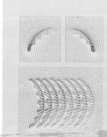

TIPS: Tilt the tool for partial impressions and adjust pressure for effect.

Stamp close impressions and adjust pressure for light to dark.

STEP 6: VEINER

This tool is often used to put veins in leaves, stems, and scrolls. It can also be used for borders and shapes. Alter the pressure and tilt the tool for different effects.

TIP: Use the "Walking the Tool" technique for smooth stamped impressions using the beveler, pear shader, and backgrounder. Practice, practice, practice! Strike

Beveler

Pear shader

Backgrounder

the tool repeatedly with a mallet or maul while moving the tool slightly to overlap the previous impression. This is done in one continuous motion to achieve a smooth, beveled line, pear-shaded fade, or background area fill.

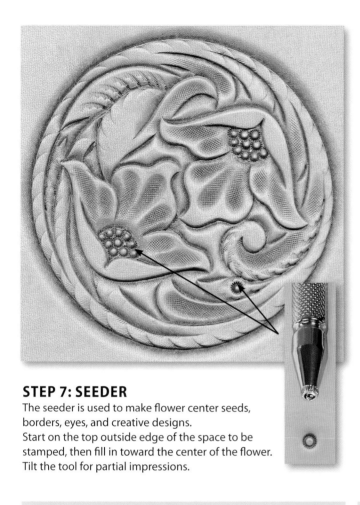

STEP 7: SEEDER

The seeder is used to make flower center seeds, borders, eyes, and creative designs.
Start on the top outside edge of the space to be stamped, then fill in toward the center of the flower.
Tilt the tool for partial impressions.

TIP: Be careful! Practice using seeders. The seeder tool's small tip end will go through the leather if too much pressure is applied during stamping.

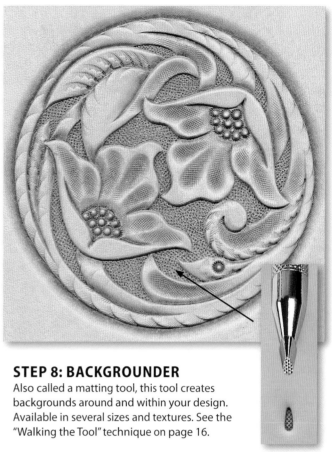

STEP 8: BACKGROUNDER

Also called a matting tool, this tool creates backgrounds around and within your design. Available in several sizes and textures. See the "Walking the Tool" technique on page 16.

TIP: Use both ends for differently sized spaces.

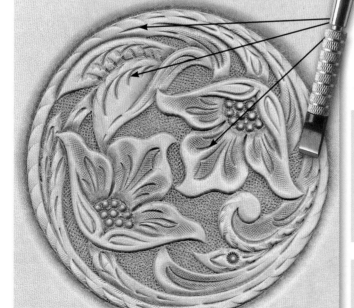

STEP 9: SWIVEL KNIFE DECORATIVE (DECO) ACCENT CUTS

These cuts add decorative accents and enhance the tooling. Practice on scrap leather (see page 13) before adding to project. Deco cuts should follow the flow of your design. Start cuts deep, then fade to the end.

TIPS: Be sure to keep your swivel knife blade stropped. (See page 13 for how to make a strop.)

If you need to stop tooling for the day, place the leather in a plastic bag. Close it and place a heavy book on top to keep the leather from drying out and curling. When you start again, re-case and continue.

TIP: Use the spoon end of a modeling tool to help form the folds and edges of petals and leaves.

MORE CARVING TECHNIQUES

The swivel knife can be used alone or combined with more tools for different and exciting effects. Here are just a few!

CARVED DESIGNS USING THE SWIVEL KNIFE AND MODELING TOOL

- Transfer your design to cased leather.
- Cut the lines using a swivel knife.
- Use the spoon end of a modeling tool to form and smooth the edges of select elements of the design.
- Use a beveler on one or both sides of the cut lines to emphasize the design.
- Use a background or matting stamp to add depth to your tooling design.
- Add a border using different stamps to frame your design.

See pages 22–27 for embossing, coloring, and finishing techniques.

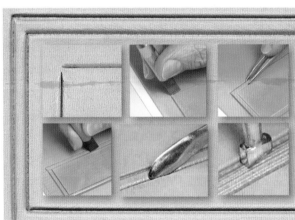

BEAD BORDER

1. Cut the first line with a swivel knife and straight edge. Stop before you get to the corners to prevent overcuts.
2. Use the tip of a swivel knife to complete the corners.
3. Run a wing divider in the cut to mark the second line to be cut. Then cut the second line with a swivel knife.
4. Use the spoon end of a modeling tool to form rounded "beads" in between the cut lines.

Optional Textured Bead: Drag the tip of a lined beveler along each side of the bead.

Inverted carving technique (see page 46)

OTHER SWIVEL KNIFE DESIGNS

- Cut the lines using a swivel knife as shown on this Celtic tooling, belt, and buckle.
- Add dimension with a modeling tool, beveler, and backgrounder.

TIPS: Keep your swivel knife stropped and leather cased to prevent the blade from dragging, causing uneven cuts and possible errors. Always practice your cuts on scrap leather.

EDGE TREATMENTS AND MORE

See pages 25–27 for coloring techniques.

There are many edge-finishing techniques and specialized tools available to achieve a professional look for your leather projects.

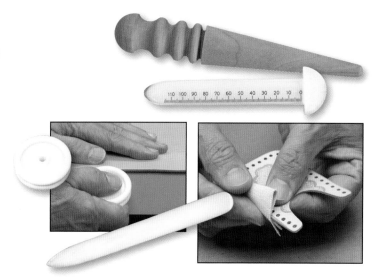

HOW TO CUT AND FINISH EDGES

1. Carefully cut out the piece using a sharp craft knife blade on a self-healing cutting mat. Keep the cuts as smooth as possible (not choppy).

2. Lightly dampen the cut edge with water, then use your choice of edge bevelers or slickers (shown below). Hold the piece or place it on a work surface for support.

3. Carefully apply edge color paints (dye or acrylic paint) by using a small wool dauber or sponge brush. Prop the piece off the work surface to dry completely. Then apply a final (acrylic) finish to the entire piece.

Edge Bevelers

For a professional look, edge bevelers are used to round and make edges more uniform. They are normally available in three sizes: for under 5 oz. weights, for 5 to 8 oz. weights, and for larger than 8 oz. weight leathers. Metal ferrules add strength to the tool. Most are pre-sharpened and ready to use.

Different Types of Edge Slickers

Wood Spindle Slicker
Burnishes (darkens) edges. A variety of grooves will fit most leather weights. Its round shape is suitable for embossing, forming, and creasing. Either end can be used.

Edge Creaser/Folder
Use to smooth, crease, form, and burnish edges, and aids in adhering glues. Groves on the head fit several leather weights.

Circle Edge Slicker
Edge slips into a groove. Easy grip for burnishing.

Bone Folder
Originally made from bone, this folder smooths, creases, forms, and burnishes.

Canvas
Use a small piece of clean canvas on a lightly dampened edge. Rub back and forth for a burnished, polished look.

Skivers

When a lace or strap edge or end is too thick, a skiver is used to shave the leather.
- A craft knife or skiver can be used for lace.
- For larger pieces, straps, or belts, use a skiver.

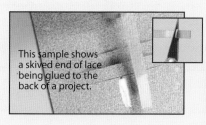

This sample shows a skived end of lace being glued to the back of a project.

When gluing a lace end to the back of a leather project, keep the end from showing through to the front by thinning it with a craft knife or skiver.

USING PUNCHES FOR DESIGNS

Create amazing designs, borders, and accents using these basic shape punches. You will need a poly board, mallet or maul, and scrap leather to test your design.

SHAPE PUNCHES
These punches are pre-sharpened and made of sturdy steel. Most are suitable for light- to medium-weight leathers.
- Natural, dyed, prefinished, and pre-embossed leathers can be punched.
- Leather does not need to be cased.

ROUND PUNCHES
Many individuals and sets are available for round hole punches.
- Round punches are normally used for stitching and lacing holes. However, they can also be used alone or with other punches and tools to create amazing designs and decorative borders.

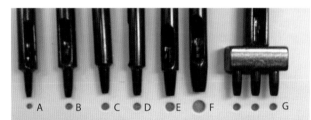

A. 1.2 mm
B. 1.5 mm
C. 1.8 mm
D. 2.1 mm
E. 3.0 mm
F. 3.6 mm
G. 1.5 mm x 3

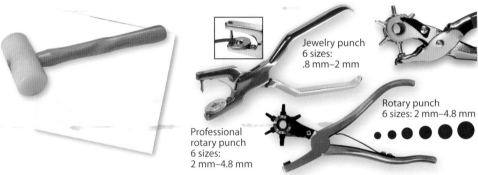

Jewelry punch
6 sizes:
.8 mm–2 mm

Professional
rotary punch
6 sizes:
2 mm–4.8 mm

Rotary punch
6 sizes: 2 mm–4.8 mm

USING PUNCHES
You will need:
- Poly cutting/punching board
- Mallet or maul

As with stamps, hold the punch straight up and down, and strike firmly with a mallet held directly over the punch.

HAND ROTARY PUNCHES
These are used for punching small holes.
- Natural, dyed, prefinished, and pre-embossed leathers can be punched.
- Leather does not need to be cased.
- Position, and then squeeze tightly until the punch pierces the leather.
- For firm leather, squeeze tightly while moving the handle left and right.

For heavier-weight leathers, use round punches (shown above).

ADD A BACKING TO YOUR PUNCHED DESIGN
- Place a piece of suede or other prefinished leather or material behind your punched design.
- Accent with hair-on leather, suede, metallics, and colored paper.

TIP: Always plan and practice punching your design on scrap leather or cardboard before punching your project.

CREATING PATTERNS

You will need:

- Pencil
- Vellum drawing paper
- Mallet or maul
- Awl or stylus
- Round templates and ruler
- Practice scrap leather
- Poly punching board

1. Trace the edge of your project onto vellum for a border design, or the area you want to fill with a punched design.

2. Test the shape and round punches you have to use for your project so you can see the sizes.

3. For curved or round designs, use a template to draw guidelines for your punched shapes. Then sketch your pattern.

4. Place the vellum pattern over scrap leather and mark the center for each punch with an awl through the pattern into the leather. Then test punch the design.

5. Transfer final pattern onto your project leather with a stylus.

TIP: Use painter's masking tape (with light adhesion) to hold the pattern in place when you transfer your design.

LEATHER APPLIQUÉS

Whether you are making little suede camp kits, jewelry, decorative frames, boxes, portfolios, or creating elaborate wall plaques with logos, monograms, or more, leather appliqués will add depth and dimension to your project.

You will need:

- Poly cutting board
- Craft knife
- Leathercraft Cement

1. Plan your design for multiple layers.

2. Be sure your cuts are as smooth as possible.

3. Finish the edges of your appliqués before cementing them onto your project (see page 19).

APPLIQUÉD KEY CADDIE

1. Cement appliqué #1 on the top of the base, which can be leather covered or painted.

2. Cement appliqué #2 on the top of dried appliqué #1.

3. Cement the belting to the long sides and trim. Repeat with the short ends. Optional: Add tacks.

See pages 22–24 for forming and Embossing instructions.

1

2

3

Base

FORMING, MOLDING, AND EMBOSSING LEATHER

Forming leather is fun! It's like playing with clay. Most weights of veg-tan leather and rawhide can be formed.

FORMING LEATHER BOWLS

You will need:

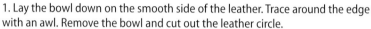

- 6 to 9 oz. Veg-tan leather
- Nonmetal bowl
- Craft knife
- Awl
- Edge beveler
- Bone folder/slicker

1. Lay the bowl down on the smooth side of the leather. Trace around the edge with an awl. Remove the bowl and cut out the leather circle.

2. Decide if you want the tooled design on the inside or outside of your finished bowl, and tool the design. Round the edges with an edge beveler and burnish with a bone folder or slicker.

3. After tooling is completed, remoisten the leather and press it into a bowl shape (tooling side up if it's to appear on the inside, down if for the outside of the project).

4. When dry in bowl, remove, then add color and a leather finish to both sides.

FORMING POUCHES, HOLSTERS, BOX LIDS, ANIMAL HEADS, AND MORE

- **To form holsters, and knife or flashlight pouches:** Wrap the gun, knife, or flashlight in plastic. Assemble the parts. Moisten the leather on the outside and inside, insert the gun, knife, or other item, and let the leather dry on the item. Then remove item, color, and add a finish.

- **To form box lids, trays, decorative shapes, animal heads, etc.:** Moisten the leather and use your fingers, modeling tool spoons, or bone folders to form the shape you want. Let the leather dry, then color and add a finish.

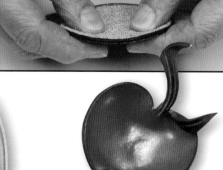

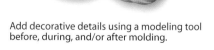

Add decorative details using a modeling tool before, during, and/or after molding.

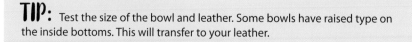

TIP: Test the size of the bowl and leather. Some bowls have raised type on the inside bottoms. This will transfer to your leather.

This jewelry box lid sample shows a background texture around the plug-embossed shapes. After completing the plug embossing, remoisten the leather. Add texture to the background using a backgrounder stamp.

EMBOSSING YOUR TOOLED DESIGN PROJECT

Plug Embossing Technique

- Cut pieces of medium- to heavyweight veg-tan into shapes (plugs). Skive the edges to help form the shape.
- Cement the plug shape onto a base (cardboard, wood, or leather). Apply contact cement over the plug and base.
- Apply contact cement on the back of thin top leather. Dampen the front side of the top leather, then carefully form/outline the plug through the top leather using the spoon end of a modeling tool.
- Optional: For additional emphasis, use a beveler around the shape.
- Embossed shape may also be cut out with a craft knife and used as an appliqué.

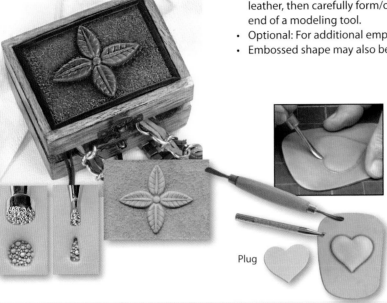

Plug

TIP: PRE-EMBOSSED VEG-TAN

Pre-embossing means that a die plate was made of a design, then a machine pressed it into cased leather. This is done to mass produce a design. Pre-embossed veg-tan leather pieces can then be colored and a finish applied for your personal touch.

Supporting Your Molded Piece

To protect your molded piece from accidentally being "pushed in" through use, back it with carpet padding.

1. Cut a piece of padding, then skive the edges to fit inside your molded lid shape.
2. Apply Leathercraft Cement on the padding and place it on the box top's base.
3. Apply cement to the back of the formed leather and position the leather over the padding. Line up the edges and press in place. Hold until the cement has dried and parts are secure.

1

2

3

FORMING RAWHIDE

Possibly one of the most historic forms of treated animal skin is rawhide. It is used for drum tops, armor, saddle trees, braided tack, pouches, and more. Native Americans and early pioneers used rawhide bindings in home and furniture construction because of its strength.

To form rawhide, you must first soften it in water.

- Cut rawhide shapes, lace, straps, etc., then place in a water bath. They will soften quickly.
- Stretch the rawhide over frames, bind parts together, or form into shapes. Let dry. It will shrink and tighten.
- You can add color dye to the water bath or paint after it is dry.

This shows an appliquéd, tooled top piece on a leather-covered plaque (see page 21).

COVERING OBJECTS WITH LEATHER

Frames, boxes, plaques, cabinetry made from medium-density fiberboard (MDF), pine or hardwoods, and even heavy cardboard can be covered with very lightweight veg-tan leather.

You will need:

- Base
- 2–3 oz. Veg-tan leather
- Craft knife
- Bone folder

1. Cut enough to cover the front and sides of a base (MDF or wood). Use contact cement on both the back of the leather and front of the board.
2. When the cement has lost its shine, it's time to adhere the board onto the back of the leather.
3. Dampen the grain side of the leather. Then apply cement to the edges of the board and carefully form, mold, and pull to cover the board.
4. Trim any excess. Form and adhere the leather to the edges with a bone folder.
5. You can then tool the front, leave it plain, or add appliqués. Work slowly and carefully. Don't pull too hard. If you are working with a base that has points, these could poke through the leather.

FORMING LEATHER MASKS

Make fun wearable or wall decor masks out of light- to medium-weight veg-tan leather.

You will need:

- 3–6 oz. Veg-tan leather
- Craft knife
- Vellum
- Scissors
- Foam head
- Water and sponge

1. Sketch or trace a pattern onto paper. Transfer to scrap leather and test your pattern.
2. Lightly dampen the leather and place on your face or a foam head. Press to form around the nose and cheeks.
3. Test the eye hole placement.
4. Remove, flatten, and use as a final pattern for your mask.
5. Let the leather dry, then color and add a finish.
The fringe on this sample was cut from the same piece as the mask.

Additional ornaments and extensions can be glued, riveted, or stitched on after the basic mask is formed.

Foam heads are available at most craft stores.

COLORING AND FINISHING LEATHER

Adding color can make all the difference in the appearance of your project. Choose dyes, stains, acrylics, or permanent markers, or leave it natural.

Leather, like wood, needs to have its natural oils refreshed or maintained using conditioners and protective finishes. If color is applied, the finish will also help seal and preserve your coloring effects.

TWO WAYS TO PROTECT LEATHER

1. Apply a leather conditioner regularly. This process works especially well for utility leathers that are exposed to the elements or heavy wear, such as belts, straps, harnesses, reins, etc.
2. Protect the leather (natural and dyed) using a lacquer, wax, or acrylic leather finish, available in high gloss, satin, or matte.

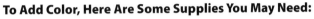

To Add Color, Here Are Some Supplies You May Need:

- Bowl of water
- Paint palettes/small bowls
- Paper towels
- Brushes (1 for each color group)
- Wool daubers
- Eye droppers

- Dyes (water-based or alcohol)
- Acrylic paints
- Permanent markers
- Scrap leather (same as project)
- Brown paper (to protect work surface)
- Sprayers (aerosol or airbrush)

- Spray booth or box shield
- Props (for positioning during coloring)
- Other applicators (for different effects)

TIPS: Set up a separate coloring/finishing area away from your tooling surface. As much as you try not to spill dyes or finishes, it will happen. Any color remaining on your tooling surface could ruin your next project. Avoid dipping a brush or dauber directly into bottles. Instead, transfer dyes to a palette or small bowls using an eyedropper. This will prevent spills and help keep dyes from drying out.

BASIC COLORING TECHNIQUES

Background Coloring

1. You must use a high-quality, fine-point brush to do background coloring.
2. Transfer dye to a palette to avoid drips. Load the brush, and touch the tip to a paper towel to remove excess dye and avoid drips.

TIP: Always begin background dyeing in the center of a space, then work up to an edge. Be sure the brush is not overloaded with dye.

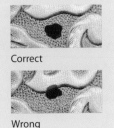

Correct

Wrong

OVERALL COLORING WITH LEATHER DYES

Overall coloring can be the only color you apply to a project or the base coat for antiques, or used for special effects. The leather needs to be dry before applying color. Some dyes will stain your hands, so wear protective gloves.

Small Projects

- For small projects (key fobs, coin purses, wristbands), you can use a wool dauber to apply the dye.
- Apply dye with a dauber in a continuous, circular, overlapping motion. Cover the entire area to be dyed at one time. Let dry, then repeat until the color is even.

Medium to Large Projects

- To obtain streak-free, overall color on medium to large projects, use an airbrush or aerosol sprayer. A dye booth (with an exhaust fan) is ideal, or a homemade cardboard spray shield works well. Always spray outside (out of the wind) or in a well-ventilated area.

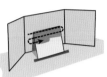

1. Prop up the leather to be dyed. You don't want it sitting in pooled dye.
2. Start spraying off to the side (never directly over leather). Work slowly, with overlapping strokes.
3. Spray one coat, pause, turn the leather, and spray again. Keep turning and spraying for even coverage and to get the color you want.

Leather sheen finish as a resist

Acrylic paint as a resist

RESIST COLORING

When you resist parts of your design with leather finishes or acrylic paints, the dye will not penetrate as deeply as on unresisted areas. This will create multitones when stain is applied.

1. Leather needs to be dry before applying.
2. Use a fine-point brush to apply a finish or acrylic paints to the design areas you want resisted (to pop out after staining). Let dry.
3. Apply multiple coats of resists, depending on the effect you want.
4. Apply a stain over the entire project. Remove any excess. Buff with a cloth.

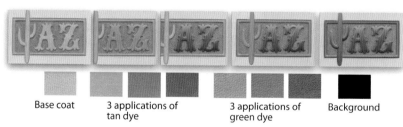

| Base coat | 3 applications of tan dye | | | 3 applications of green dye | | Background |

TIP: Always start with light colors and then use dark colors. Once color is applied, it cannot be removed. It's very much like working with watercolors. Start light and repeat the application to create the color you want.

SHADING FOR DIMENSION

- Leather dyes can be diluted. If you're using a water-based dye, use water. If it's an alcohol-based dye, use a solvent.
- Test the colors on scrap leather (same as the project leather).
- Dip the brush in the dye, touch the paper towel or scrap leather to remove excess dye, and form a point.
- Work slowly and carefully with each color.
- See the steps below for shading techniques.

(Note: Apply dye to the background area first or last.)

1. Apply the base coat (always a light color). Solid yellow dye is shown above.
2. Mix shades of your colors, from light to full strength. Test them on scrap leather.
3. Apply one shade at a time, starting with the lightest shade (hue).
4. Slowly overlap strokes to build up the colors you want, where you want.
5. Let the dye dry between applications, so you can see the actual color. Reapply where needed.

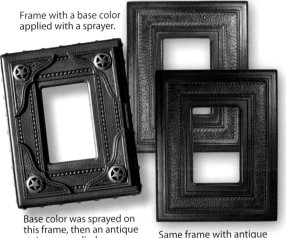

Frame with a base color applied with a sprayer.

Base color was sprayed on this frame, then an antique stain was applied.

Same frame with antique applied over the base color.

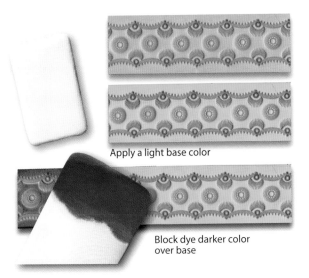

Apply a light base color

Block dye darker color over base

One-Step

ANTIQUE STAIN COLORING

- Antique stains come in paste or liquid form and may be applied over natural or dyed leather.
- Be sure the leather is completely dry before applying.
- Shown at right is a frame "overall dye colored," and then an antique stain was applied.

1. Apply an antique stain over natural or dyed leather, per the stain manufacturer's instructions.

2. Remove excess with a sponge, soft cloth, or piece of sheep's wool. Buff, let the leather dry completely, then apply a protective leather finish.

BLOCK DYEING

This technique uses a wooden block wrapped in white cotton cloth, dipped in leather dye, and stroked over a tooled surface, leaving dye on just the high points of the tooled design.

You will need:
- Hand-size wooden blocks
- Cloth
- Scissors
- Stapler

1. Cut long strips of cotton cloth (a t-shirt will work well), long enough to wrap six or more times around the block, wide enough to overlap and cover the block's ends.

2. Tightly wrap the block. Trim the cloth's ends to just overlap. Secure the ends with a stapler (with long staples). Do not staple on the large, flat sides.

- Be sure your tooling is dry before applying leather dye.
- If you want a two-toned project, first apply a light dye.
- Apply leather dye to the block and stroke over the tooled design. Repeat until you achieve the effect you want.
- Remove excess dye with a clean block, let dry, and apply a final leather finish.

ACRYLICS, PERMANENT MARKERS, AND MORE

- Use acrylic paints and permanent markers for accents on your coloring projects.
- Experiment with different applicators (sponges, rolled cloth, combs, brushes, feathers, ink stamps) to create special effects.

TIPS: For best results, use a high-quality, fine-point brush for detail work (#4 Round Red Sable is shown here). Have separate brushes for different color groups: reds, blues, greens, yellows, blacks, browns, and finishes. Once dye seeps down into a brush's ferrule, it is hard to get out. It could reappear and ruin your next project.

ONE-STEP (STAIN AND LEATHER FINISH)

One-Step is a light stain and leather finish combined. Apply it to undyed or colored leather.

1. When the leather is dry, apply One-Step with a slightly damp sponge.

2. Rub it with a sponge to remove any excess, let it dry, and then buff.

An additional finish is not needed, since it is included in this One-Step stain/finish.

BASIC STITCHING, LACING, AND BRAIDING

Waxed thread, lace, and leather cord are used to assemble leather projects. The method of lacing, stitching, and braiding you choose can be functional as well as decorative.

NEEDLE FOR WAXED THREAD

Stitching Needle

There are two ways to thread the needle:
1. Pierce the thread and push the needle through the opening.
2. Or just twist the end around the lace.

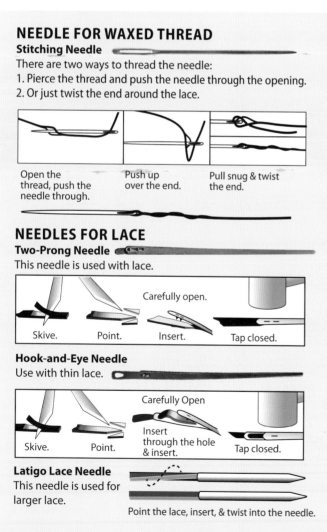

Open the thread, push the needle through.

Push up over the end.

Pull snug & twist the end.

NEEDLES FOR LACE

Two-Prong Needle

This needle is used with lace.

Skive. Point. Carefully open. Insert. Tap closed.

Hook-and-Eye Needle

Use with thin lace.

Skive. Point. Carefully Open. Insert through the hole & insert. Tap closed.

Latigo Lace Needle

This needle is used for larger lace.

Point the lace, insert, & twist into the needle.

GENERAL TOOLS

Stylus/Modeling Tools: Use for scribing stitch lines, and pulling thread and lace tight.

Wing Dividers: Use for scribing stitch lines.

Rotary Punch: For punching round lacing or stitching holes.

Craft Knife, Snips, and Scissors: Use the size best suited for your projects.

Awl: For punching small holes and for making repairs.

Masking Tape/Leathercraft Cement: For securing lace and holding.

Vellum: For making patterns.

Ruler/Straight Edge: For measuring and for using as a guide.

Mallet, Maul, and Poly Board: Use either a mallet or maul and a protective board for punching.

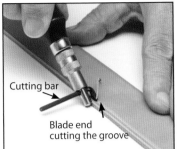

Cutting bar

Blade end cutting the groove

TOOLS FOR STITCHING AND LACING

Stitching Groover

This tool is used for measuring and making grooves for hand stitching. The cutting bar is adjustable. To use, position the tool next to the edge of the leather and pull toward you.

TIP: Hand stitching that is countersunk into a groove created by a stitching groover will last longer because it is protected from wear.

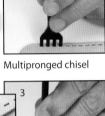

Single & multi-round punches

Multipronged chisel

Punches and Chisels

Round punches are available with a single tube or multiple tubes and in many sizes for stitching and lacing holes. Thonging chisels are available in single-pronged and multipronged, straight or angled, configurations, and are offered in ³⁄₃₂" or ⅛" to match common lace sizes. Use with a mallet or maul and a poly board.

1. First scribe or groove a guideline for the holes.
2. Use a multipronged punch or chisel for straight rows.
3. Use a single-pronged punch or chisel for corners and curved lines.

TIP: Use a stylus and a straight edge to scribe guidelines for straight rows and a wing divider to scribe around corners.

Overstitch Wheels

This tool creates uniform marks for hand stitching. It is also used to run back over stitches to make them uniform. An overstitch wheel can also be used alone to simulate stitching for border designs.

TIP: There are three ways to guide the overstitch wheel:

1. First use a stitching groover to create a guide channel in the leather.
2. Use a wing divider to scribe a very light guideline.
3. Run the wheel along a straight edge ruler.

Push the tool along the groove made by the stitching groover

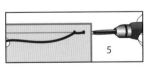

Small   Medium   Large

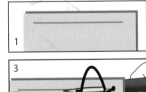

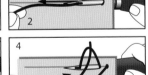

Speedy Stitcher

For repairs, this tool will create a lockstitch using waxed thread. Best suited for heavy leathers and canvas.

1. Lightly scribe a guideline or make a groove for stitching on both parts.
2. Push the needle through both parts on the guidelines. Draw out twice as much thread as needed for the length of line to be stitched.
3. Hold the thread and pull the needle back out of hole 1 and into hole 2. Pull the needle out of the hole enough to form a loop.
4. Pass all thread through the loop.
5. Hold the thread taut, pull the needle out to form a lockstitch (see the Tip). Continue stitching.

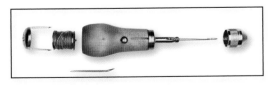

TIP: The finished lockstitch should go between the parts, not on the surfaces (front or back).

Cross-section
Part
Part

STITCHING, LACING, AND BRAIDING TECHNIQUES

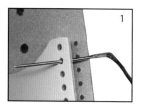
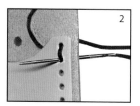
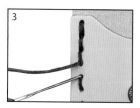
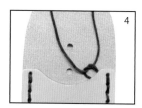

Running Stitch

Also called a "straight stitch," it can be done in and out in one direction or turned and stitched back to fill in between previous stitches.

1. Begin between parts. Stitch out through the front part of hole #2. Leave 3" of thread to tie off later.
2. Stitch through aligned holes #1. Pull tight. Stitch back through aligned holes #2.
3. Stitch twice through the last hole, turn, and stitch back around filling in between the previous stitches.
4. End between the parts, tie the thread ends in a knot, and trim the thread.

TIP: When stitching back around a project filling in between previous stitches, always stitch up and down the holes on the same side of the previous stitch.

Correct

Wrong

Cross-Stitch

Join the parts or seams, or use purely as a decorative border. Here are just a few ways to do cross-stitches. Use needles for easier stitching. Some lace can be cut into points if the stitching holes are large.

A. To Stitch One Cross-Stitch:

1. Beginning on the back side, stitch out hole #1 and into #4.
2. Stitch out #3 and into #2.
3. Tie the ends in a knot on the back. Trim the excess.

B. To Stitch Several Cross-Stitches:

1. Start on the back going out hole #1. Leave several inches to tie off at the end.
2. Stitch one direction to the end, turn, and stitch back making the crosses.
3. Tie the ends in a knot on the back. Trim the excess.

C. Another Way to Stitch Several Cross-Stitches:

1. Fold the thread in half. Stitch out holes #1 and #2, positioning the center of the thread between the holes on back.
2. Cross the threads, go down the next holes, cross on the back, and go out the same holes. Repeat to the end.
3. Tie the ends in a knot on the back.

Whip Stitch

The whip stitch is a very popular and efficient way to join parts and decorate edges. It works well with either lace or waxed thread.

Mirrored Whip Stitch   Double Whip Stitch

Stitch one direction, turn, and stitch back.

Variations:

1. Begin between the parts. Leave the end between the parts.
2. Pull tight catching end and continue.
3. Stitch over the edges and continue.
4. End between the parts, pull tight, and trim the lace.

TIP: Pull the stitches tight as you go. Keep the lace flat; do not twist.

Box Stitch

This stitch is often used to attach a belt loop to a holster, belt bag, knife pouch, or sheath.
1. Punch six holes as shown.
2. Begin between the parts out hole #1, down #2, and continue.
3. Back at hole #1, turn and go back around (#1 to #6, etc.).
4. End between the parts, tie a knot between the parts, and trim the thread.

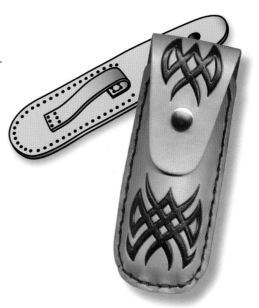

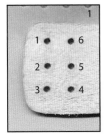

Single-Needle Baseball Stitch

Use waxed thread and this stitch to repair a baseball, make a footbag, or sew pillow and garment seams.

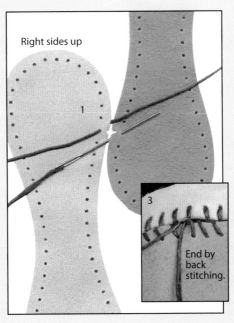

Right sides up

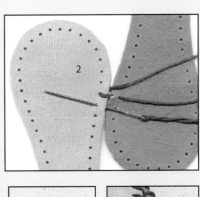

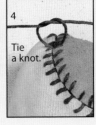

End by back stitching.

Tie a knot.

Push the knot to the inside.

Double-Needle Baseball Stitch

All Major League baseballs are hand cross-stitched using two needles and waxed thread. Wax is used to stiffen the thread, allowing for easier stitching and longer life of the seam.

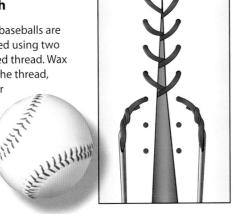

These stitching techniques are used on a baseball glove:

Whip Stitch

Cross Stitch

Running Stitch

Whip Stitch

Creative Buckstitching

Buckstitching is more than the traditional Western border technique. It offers many different styles and creative options. It is widely used for binding and decorative borders but can be combined with alternate chisel lacing techniques for special effects.

Buckstitch with slits punched with a straight chisel.

Buckstitch with slits punched with an angled chisel.

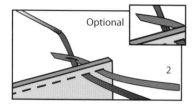
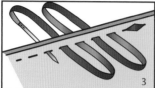
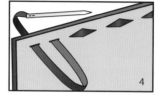

Basic Diamond Buckstitching Steps

1. Prepare your project for buckstitching by scribing guidelines where the stitching will be, using a stylus.
For round corners, use a wing divider. These steps apply to using an angled chisel as well. Attach the lace to a two-pronged needle.
2. From the back, stitch out the first hole. Leave the end to tuck under or pierce with the next stitch.
3. Continue. Pull the lace tight after a few stitches.
4. Pull the last stitch through the last holes.
5. On the back, stitch under the previous stitch. Pull tight and cut the lace.

TIP: Always pre-punch slits for your designs by using single-pronged or multipronged punches and chisels. Some are straight and some are angled.

Variations

Many different designs can be created using chisels and lace.

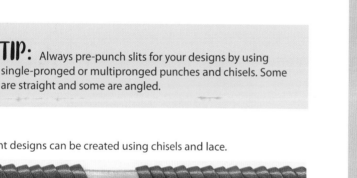

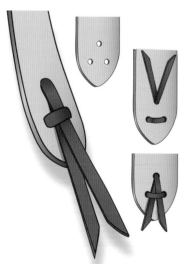

Hitch Stitches

These stitches are used to attach handles and straps to bags.

Three-Hole Slip Hitch
1. Punch three holes as shown.
2. Lace into the bottom two holes.
3. Then lace out the top hole.
4. Tuck the ends under the loop and pull tight.
5. Trim the ends.

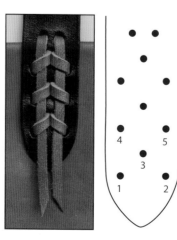

Herringbone Slip Hitch
1. Mark and punch holes as shown.
2. Starting from the back, lace out #1 and #2. Pull so the lace center is between #1 and #2.
3. Push both lace ends through #3, then out #4 and #5.
4. Repeat in and out to the top.
5. Lace out the top two holes then down under the diagonal stitches.
6. Pull all stitches tight and trim the ends.

Classic Double-Loop Lacing

This technique can be used to join parts (as shown below), wrap buckles, and create decorative edging. Holes can be punched with either round or chisel punches, and there can be an even or odd number of holes.

 **1** Start and leave ¾".

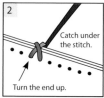 **2** Turn the end up.

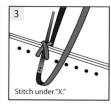 **3** Stitch under "X."

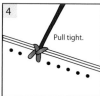 **4** Pull tight.

 **5** Stitch through the next holes.

6 Stitch under "X."

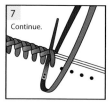 **7** Continue.

8 Double stitch 3 corner holes.

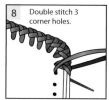 **9** Add lace. 6" #1 #2 ¾" When 6" of lace is left, add second needle.

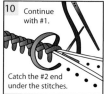 **10** Continue with #1. Catch the #2 end under the stitches.

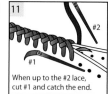 **11** #2 #1 When up to the #2 lace, cut #1 and catch the end.

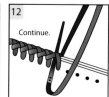 **12** Continue.

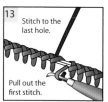 **13** Stitch to the last hole. Pull out the first stitch.

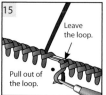 **14** Pull the lace out of the hole.

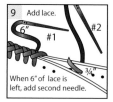 **15** Leave the loop. Pull out of the loop.

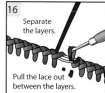 **16** Separate the layers. Pull the lace out between the layers.

 **17** Pull tight. Cut the end. Tuck the end under the next stitches.

18 Continue.

 **19** Stitch through the open loop. Pull tight.

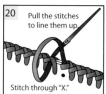 **20** Pull the stitches to line them up. Stitch through "X."

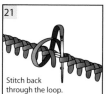 **21** Stitch back through the loop.

 **22** Stitch into the last hole and out between the layers.

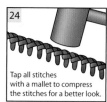 **23** Pull tight and trim close to the lace.

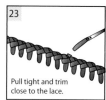 **24** Tap all stitches with a mallet to compress the stitches for a better look.

TIP: You can decorate leather projects using classic embroidery stitches. Here are just a few.

Prep: Plan your designs, make patterns, and transfer them to the leather. For thread, use an awl for making holes in the leather. For lace and larger holes, use round punches with a mallet and poly board.

Daisy Stitch
1. From the back, stitch out and back down hole #1 forming a loop (petal).
2. Stitch out and back down #2 catching the top of the loop.

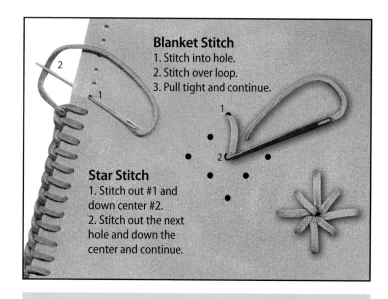

Blanket Stitch
1. Stitch into hole.
2. Stitch over loop.
3. Pull tight and continue.

Star Stitch
1. Stitch out #1 and down center #2.
2. Stitch out the next hole and down the center and continue.

TIP: Secure the ends on the back either under a stitch or with Leathercraft Cement.

LANYARD SQUARE BRAID
Use plastic or leather lace.

TIP: Be sure to keep the lace flat (not twisted) during braiding. Pull the lace tight after each stitch.

The Square Braid

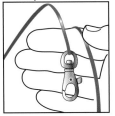

1. Wrap the first lace loosely around your index finger and position the hook.

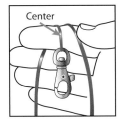

Center

2. Hold with your fingers. Position the lace centers.

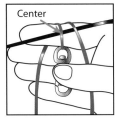

Center

3. Slip the second lace under the first lace. Line up the centers.

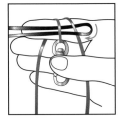

4. Bend the right end of the second lace down, go over, and then under the first lace.

5. Bend the left end (second lace) up, over, and under the first lace.

6. Slip your finger out. Pull the ends to tighten the braid.

7. This completes the first square braid.

8. Bend the top lace down, forming a loop.

9. Bend the bottom lace up, forming a loop.

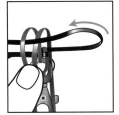

10. Bend the right end of the second lace, over and under the loops.

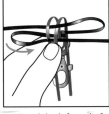

11. Bend the left end of the same lace over and under the loops.

12. Slowly pull the ends to tighten the braid.

13. Continue as in Steps 8–12 to reach the desired length.

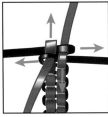

14. To end with a Turk's Knot, first loosen the **last** braid.

15. Wrap one lace end around to the corner (where the laces cross).

Under Both

16. Insert the lace end under both crossed laces, and up/out the center of the braid.

17. Pull the lace end out of the center to tighten the stitch. Continue on the other corners.

18. Trim the lace ends to the desired length with scissors or a craft knife.

The Spiral Braid
Start by following Steps 1–7 above, then skip to Spiral Step 8 below.

Spiral Step 8. Bend the top lace diagonally down, forming a loop.

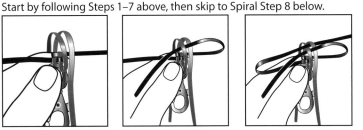

Spiral Step 9. Bend the bottom lace diagonally up, forming a loop.

Spiral Step 10. Bend the right end of the second lace over and under the loops.

Spiral Step 11. Bend the left end of the same lace over and under the loops.

Spiral Step 12. Continue braiding the spiral. After a completed braid, you can switch back to the square braid, or end by following Steps 14–18 to do the Turk's Knot.

Braid for Cuff Bracelets and Watchbands

This flat braid technique is designed to be tough and also decorative. You can use prefinished leather, pre-embossed leather with a design, or natural veg-tan leather that can be dyed or stained to your liking.

Size the pattern to fit your bracelet blank or watchband. For more than one braid, the number of slits should be in multiples of five.

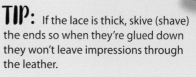

TIP: If the lace is thick, skive (shave) the ends so when they're glued down they won't leave impressions through the leather.

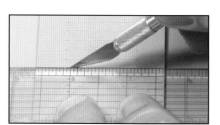

1. Cut the lines with a craft knife.

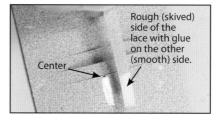

Center

Rough (skived) side of the lace with glue on the other (smooth) side.

2. Apply glue on one end of the lace.

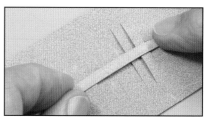

3. Hold down until the glue sets.

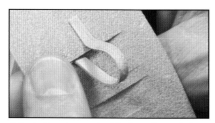

4. Push the other end of the lace through the first slit.

5. Pull the lace through the first slit to the front side.

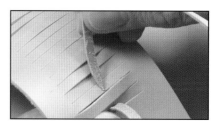

6. On the front, push the lace end through the third slit.

7. Push the lace end out slit #2 and back thru #1.

8. Pull to form a loop.

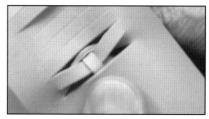

9. Continue over and down into slit #1.

3
2
1

10. Bring the end out slit #3.

5
4
3

11. Next, go down #5, out #4, and down

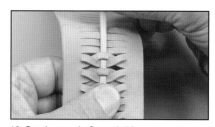

12. Continue, as in Steps 6–10.

13. Finish on the back. Trim the lace.

14. Apply glue to the lace and leather.

15. Hold in position until the glue sets.

Mystery Braid

This is a classic, timeless technique. It works well for wristbands, watchbands, straps, holders, and more.

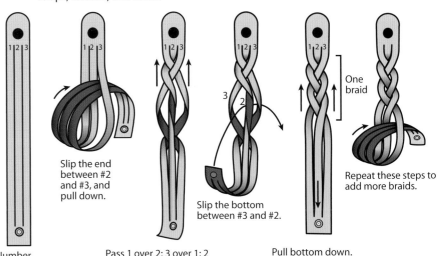

Number the strands.

Slip the end between #2 and #3, and pull down.

Pass 1 over 2; 3 over 1; 2 over 3 and push up.

Slip the bottom between #3 and #2.

Pull bottom down. Work braid up to top.

One braid

Repeat these steps to add more braids.

TIP: Remember "under two and over one."

Four-Strand Round Braid

- Cut lace lengths three times the desired finished length.
- Use the same or different colored strands of lace.
- Use a swivel hook, key ring, or first braided loop.
- For easier braiding, loop over a hook or nail.
- Keep the lace flat, and pull the braids snug as you go.
- Finish with a knot, or tie off with waxed thread.

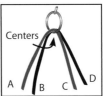

Centers

1. Arrange the strands as shown.

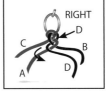

2. Pass C under B.

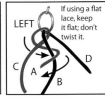

If using a flat lace, keep it flat; don't twist it.

LEFT

3. Pass the top left strand A behind C and B, and then back over B.

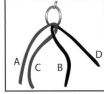

RIGHT

4. Pass the top right strand D behind A and B, and then back over A.

5. Repeat on the left side: pass the top left strand behind the bottom left and right strands, then back over the bottom right strand. Pull snug.

6. Repeat on the right side: pass the top right strand down behind the bottom right and left strands, then back over the bottom left strand.

7. Continue until you reach the desired length. Tie off.

Survival Braid

This braid is strong and secure, and it works well with round leather lace or paracord.

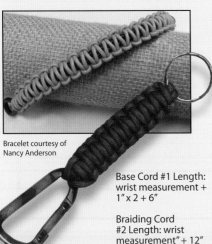

Bracelet courtesy of Nancy Anderson

Base Cord #1 Length: wrist measurement + 1" x 2 + 6"

Braiding Cord #2 Length: wrist measurement" + 12"

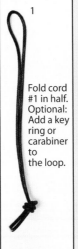

1 Fold cord #1 in half. Optional: Add a key ring or carabiner to the loop.

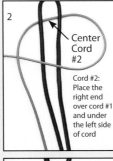

2 Center Cord #2

Cord #2: Place the right end over cord #1 and under the left side of cord

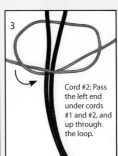

3 Cord #2: Pass the left end under cords #1 and #2, and up through the loop.

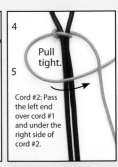

4 Pull tight.

5 Cord #2: Pass the left end over cord #1 and under the right side of cord #2.

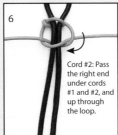

6 Cord #2: Pass the right end under cords #1 and #2, and up through the loop.

7 Pull tight. Continue braiding.

8 To finish, pull the ends back under the cords.

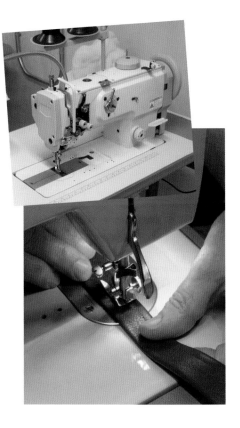

USING A SEWING MACHINE FOR LEATHER

When quick, consistent assembly is required, consider stitching with a sewing machine. If you have access to an industrial sewing machine, it will be able to handle most weights of leather. However, for lighter garment leathers, a home sewing machine can be used.

You will need:

- Scissors
- Snips
- Leathercraft Cement or rubber cement
- Masking tape (never use pins on leather)
- Mallet
- Ruler or measuring tape

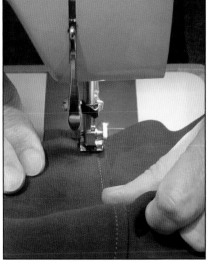

BASIC SEWING SUGGESTIONS

- Test your pattern on muslin for proper fit before transferring the pattern to leather. Removing stitches will leave visible holes, possibly ruining your leather.
- Position and tape the pattern on the back (wrong) side of the leather to avoid damaging the top. Note: Because of the thickness of leather, it cannot be folded as you would ordinarily do with fabric for a traditional pattern. Right and left sides need to be cut as one whole, flat piece.
- Use needles in sizes 11 to 16 for light- to medium-weight leathers. Leather needles are available for home sewing machines.
- Use heavy duty cotton wrapped/polyester core thread.
- Use larger stitches so the leather will not pucker while sewing. Be sure to sew slowly.

TIP: You can disguise or decorate seams using hand-laced stitches (see page 32).

TIP: Stitch the seam (right sides together), then open it on a work surface, carefully apply cement on both sides of the seam, fold, and lightly tap with a mallet to secure.

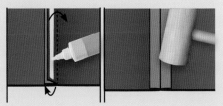

TIP: To install piping or decorative edging inside a seam, cut a length of leather that matches the length of the seam.

1. Insert cording in the fold and stitch close to the cord.

2. Position on one side of the leather and stitch together, aligning the cut edges and stitch.

3. Position the second piece and stitch. (Optional: Braid the edge of a separate strip of leather.)

Leather braid edging

Courtesy of Steel Strike Custom Leather Products

REENACTMENT COSTUMING AND ACCOUTREMENTS

Classical era people, Vikings, medieval figures, Native Americans, fur traders, Wild West folk, military personnel, mythical characters, and even superheroes all have one thing in common: leather!

The most popular leathers used in reenactments include veg-tanned leather, suedes, latigo, kangaroo, bison, deer, and calfskins, plus hair-on hides and rawhide.

Today, reenactors can use antique and modern tools, machines, dyes and finishes, plus a wide selection of leathers to create historic and educational reenactment apparel and accoutrements.

Hundreds of new and old techniques for tooling, stamping, carving, molding, hand stitching, lacing, and braiding live on.

Bone and antique brass bead necklace, bandolier, and breastplate

Brain-tan deerskin outfit and beadwork, courtesy of Tony Laier

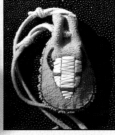

Bead and quill work on brain-tan (deerskin), courtesy of O. J. Laier

TIP: To "antique" current hardware:

1. Soak in lacquer remover for several hours.

2. Soak in "brush-on blackener for metals" (available online) to the color you want.

3. Bathe in water to neutralize. Keep away from children.

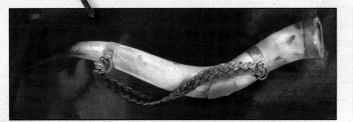

TIP: To distress or antique your leather:

1. Wrap the leather in plastic to keep it clean.

2. Pound it with chains or rocks.

3. Apply stain, antiques, or dyes.

LEATHER JEWELRY AND ACCENTS

Whether you're making new pieces or enhancing great finds and cherished heirlooms, leather accents, cording, and lace will add beauty and durability to your creations.

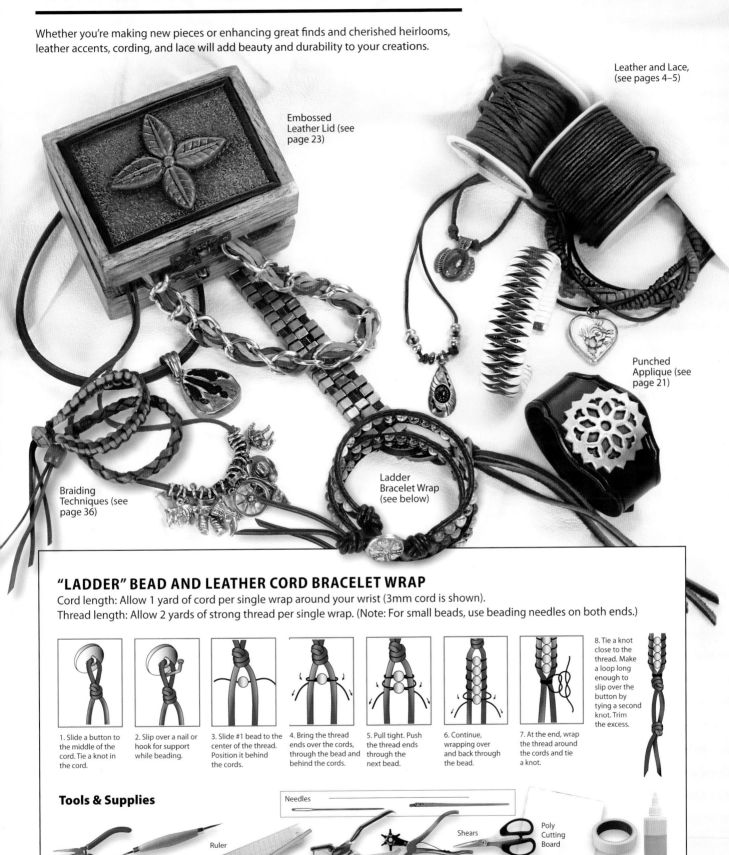

Embossed Leather Lid (see page 23)

Leather and Lace, (see pages 4–5)

Punched Applique (see page 21)

Braiding Techniques (see page 36)

Ladder Bracelet Wrap (see below)

"LADDER" BEAD AND LEATHER CORD BRACELET WRAP

Cord length: Allow 1 yard of cord per single wrap around your wrist (3mm cord is shown).
Thread length: Allow 2 yards of strong thread per single wrap. (Note: For small beads, use beading needles on both ends.)

1. Slide a button to the middle of the cord. Tie a knot in the cord.

2. Slip over a nail or hook for support while beading.

3. Slide #1 bead to the center of the thread. Position it behind the cords.

4. Bring the thread ends over the cords, through the bead and behind the cords.

5. Pull tight. Push the thread ends through the next bead.

6. Continue, wrapping over and back through the bead.

7. At the end, wrap the thread around the cords and tie a knot.

8. Tie a knot close to the thread. Make a loop long enough to slip over the button by tying a second knot. Trim the excess.

Tools & Supplies

Needles

Pliers

Modeling Tools

Ruler

Craft Knife

Jewelry Punch

Rotary Hole Punch

Shears

Awl

Poly Cutting Board

Tape & Cements

INSTALLING HARDWARE

Whether for assembly, decoration, or utility, installing proper hardware adds that final touch that can make or break your project. Here are some helpful tips and how-to's.

BUCKLES

Installation Options

1. For heel and center bars: You first need to punch a slot for the buckle tongue (prong). See the tip below.
2. To secure the belt on the bar and trophy buckles:
A. Rivets (plain or decorative) for permanent attachment
B. Snaps (plain or decorative) for easy removal
C. Post screws for easy removal (see page 44 for installation of rivets, snaps, and post screws)
D. Stitching: This includes hand or machine stitching, or the Speedy Stitcher, for permanent attachment. (See pages 28–37 for stitching techniques.)
3. Clip-on: This style of buckle clamps on the belt end like a binder clip.

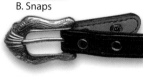

A. Rivets

B. Snaps

C. Post screws

Center bar

Heel bar

D. Hand or machine stitched

Clip-on

Trophy

TIP: To punch the buckle tongue slot, use an oblong bag punch (shown) or:

1. Punch two round holes.
2. Connect the holes and cut with a craft knife.

METAL D-RINGS AND RECTANGLES

D-ring and rectangle loops can be used instead of a buckle and as keepers.
• Install along with buckles.
• Secure with the same installation as a buckle: with rivets, snaps, post screws, and hand or machine stitching.

Used in pairs, D-rings and rectangles become a belt or strap closure.
• Install two together on a belt or strap.
• Loop the strap through both and secure, normally with stitching.
• To use: Loop the other end of belt up through both D-rings, over the edge of the top D-ring, and down through the bottom D-ring. Pull snug.

KEEPERS: LEATHER AND METAL

Select the keeper to coordinate with your buckle and project.
• To go with a buckle: Install the keeper behind the buckle, using the same hardware (rivet, snap, post screw, or stitching).
• For decoration: Select the style and hardware of your choice.

Leather keepers are normally formed using staples, or they are hand stitched.

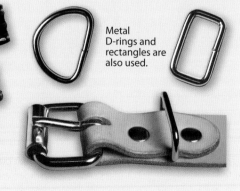

Metal D-rings and rectangles are also used.

BUTTON STUDS

A fast, simple closure for bags, wristbands, and more.

You will need:

- Button stud (2 parts)
- Round hole punch
- Buttonhole punch
- Rotary punch
- Mallet
- Poly cutting board
- Screwdriver

1. Punch a ³⁄₃₂″ single, round hole in front using a punch, mallet, and poly cutting board, or a rotary punch.

2. From the back, insert the screw part of the button stud.

3. Place the button stud on the screw and tighten with a screwdriver.

4. Fold the flap over and mark the placement for the hole. Punch the flap hole with a buttonhole punch and mallet on a poly board.

TIP: For speed and for multiple projects, a buttonhole punch is great to have. If you don't have one, use a round punch and a craft knife to cut the lower slit. Cut just a little length and test. If it's too long, your hole will not secure the stud.

CLASPS

Many clasps have prongs for installation. Here are the basic steps.

You will need:

- Four-part clasp
- Craft knife (or single thonging chisel)
- Pliers

Eyelet and back plate   Turn and back plate

TIP: Work on a soft cloth or a piece of leather to prevent damaging or scarring the clasp front.

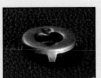

1. On the flap, trace the eyelet's inside hole and cut. Position the eyelet over the hole and press, mark the prong positions, and cut. **Bag front:** Position the turn part under the flap and eyelet hole, mark the prong positions, and cut.

2. **On the flap:** Position the clasp eyelet part over the hole and prong slits. Insert the clasp prongs into the slits.

3. Turn the flap and eyelet in position over onto a soft cloth, back side up. Place the eyelet plate inside the prongs. Bend the prongs with pliers to secure. Slip pliers between the plate and leather to crimp.

4. Insert turn clasp prongs into the slits in the front part. Turn over the resting turn clasp on a soft towel to protect the clasp.

5. On the back side, place the eyelet plate over the prongs. Bend the prongs with pliers to secure the parts. Slip pliers between the back plate and leather to crimp.

CLIPS (SPRINGS)

An alternative for a belt loop on sheaths, cell phone holders, bags, holsters, etc.

You will need:

- Round punch
- Mallet
- Craft knife
- Rivet and setter

Clips with a rivet hole do not need a bottom slot. Clips with a "bump" need a top slit and a bottom slot.

Bump

Some clips have a hole at the bottom for a rivet. A bottom slot is not needed. See page 44 for setting a rivet.

This clip style needs a bottom slot for a bump that locks the clip in position.

1. **Top slit:** Position the clip, mark the width, and punch two holes within that width. Cut a slit between the holes.

2. **Bottom slot:** Follow Step 1 above, but connect the two holes by making top and bottom cuts.

CONCHOS

Conchos come in a variety of styles with different installations.

Screw-Back Conchos

You will need:
- Punch
- Mallet
- Screwdriver

1. Punch a hole smaller than the screw's diameter.
2. Insert the concho and secure with a screw. See adapters on page 40.

Leather Conchos

With a single, center hole, they can be used with a screw-back or rivet on conchos as decoration or as spacers. See the Tip on this page.

Rivet Conchos

You will need:
- Punch
- Mallet
- Rivet and setter

See page 44.

Slotted Conchos

You will need:
- Punch
- Mallet
- Craft knife
- Lace

(See the Tip below.)

TIP: When installing a screw-back concho on a single layer of leather, you will need a spacer under it or on the project back in order for the screw to tighten properly.

1. Cut a circle of leather to match the size of your concho, or use a pre-punched leather concho.

2. Place between the concho and project leather, or on the back (inside) of the project part. Then tighten the screw.

TIP: How to Make a Bleed Knot through a Slotted Concho

1. Trace concho slots onto the project, and punch and thread the lace, pulling it until middle of the lace is between the slots. Then insert the lace through the conchos and pull tight.

2. Cut a slit in the top lace close to the slot.

3. Run the bottom lace up through the slit.

4. Cut a second slit close to the first slit.

5. Run the bottom lace through. Pull tight.

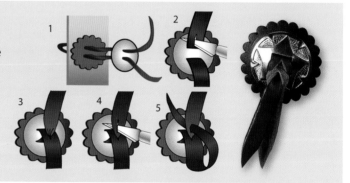

TIP: Some conchos have very sharp edges. Be very careful when working with them on your leather project parts, so they won't mark the leather. If they do, use the spoon of a modeling tool to smooth out the marks.

Concho Adapters

Use conchos in many ways, including cabinet knobs, drawer pulls, buttons, fridge magnets, and decorations.

You will need:
- Screw-back conchos
- Adapters
- Pliers

Concho knob adapter

Concho button adapter

Courtesy of Steel Strike Leather Products

Magnetic adapter

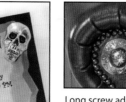

Long screw adapter

TIP: When using long screw adapters, they can be cut off if they're too long for your project depth. These adapters were used on this frame and cut off using a heavy wire cutter.

EYELETS

Eyelets are used to strengthen punched holes or as decoration.

You will need:

- Eyelet setter and anvil
- Poly cutting board
- Mallet
- Stylus or awl
- Eyelets

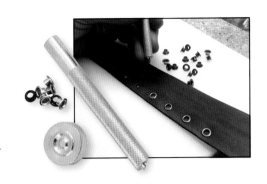

1. Mark the placement for the eyelets using a modeling tool stylus or awl.
2. Punch holes to fit the eyelet size using a punch, poly cutting board, and mallet.
3. Position the anvil (grooved side up) and place the eyelet on the anvil. Turn the leather face down onto the eyelet (on the anvil), and push the eyelet up through the hole.
4. Insert the setter and strike firmly with a mallet.

Fringe Tassel Clips

These clips make colorful accents.

You will need:

- Tassel clips
- Leather fringe
- Leathercraft Cement

TIP: Use varied colors within the same tassel for colorful accents.

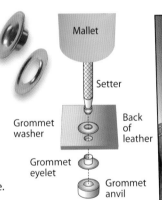  

1. Tightly roll one fringe piece onto itself. Then add a second and third piece. Cement the last edge to hold the tassel together.

2. Apply Leathercraft Cement to the inside of the tassel clip. Avoid getting cement on the outside edge.

3. Push the tassel roll into the clip base. Let the cement dry completely.

GROMMETS

Install grommets in leather or canvas to prevent holes from tearing.

You will need:

- Grommet Setter
- Anvil
- Round hole punch (slighlty smaller than grommet hole)
- Mallet
- Hard work surface

Mallet

Setter

Grommet washer

Back of leather

Grommet eyelet

Grommet anvil

Hard work surface

1. Mark where you want the grommet installed. Punch a hole in the leather. The hole should be snug fitting.
2. Push the eyelet through the hole on the finished side of the leather.
3. Place a washer over the eyelet. Position so the eyelet is resting in the anvil groove.
4. Position the setter over the eyelet edge up through the washer and strike firmly with the mallet. Repeat until grommet is set.

HOOKS AND PEGS

Turn leather plaques into useful, decorative household accessories.

You will need:

- Screw hooks
- Pegs and screws
- Small drill
- Pliers
- Screwdriver

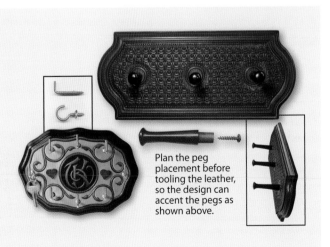

Plan the peg placement before tooling the leather, so the design can accent the pegs as shown above.

When the project is completely finished (colored, final leather finish applied and dry), then add the hardware hooks or pegs.

For hooks: Pre-drill pilot holes using a bit that is just smaller than the hook screw's diameter.

For pegs: Either glue or screw the pegs into position. For both options, you first need to drill a hole in the plaque's front for pegs. Select a bit the same size as the peg base. For the screw (through the back), select a bit a little smaller than the screw.

RINGS

These come in many sizes!
Use on handbags and backpacks:
- Join project parts, straps, and belting.
- Install with rivets, snaps, post screws, or stitching.

Use as a base for mandalas, dream catchers, and macramé:
- Wrap with suede lace or cord.

Use for mobiles, framing for a picture, and keepsake artwork:
- Join different sizes with lace.
- Add toy animals, flowers, shapes inside rings.

RIVETS

Useful and decorative!

You will need:
- Rivet setter
- Optional anvil
- Rivets
- Mallet
- Poly cutting board
- Hard work surface

TIP: Combine rivets with conchos. See page 42.

Mallet

Setter

Rivet cap

Rivet post   Optional: Anvil (flat side up)

Hard work surface

Install as permanent fasteners (attaching two pieces of leather):
- Mark the hole's placement with a stylus, awl, or pen (where they will join).
- Punch round holes with a punch and mallet on a cutting board.
- Position rivet parts as shown.
- Install with a setter, anvil, and mallet.

Install as decorative designs:
- First plan your pattern on tracing paper or vellum (see page 7). Test your pattern.
- Transfer the pattern to leather, marking holes with a stylus or awl.
- Install rivets as shown at left.

POSTS AND SCREWS

Sometimes referred to as Chicago Screws, these are removable fasteners, making them ideal for rifle slings, guitar straps, bag straps, and belt buckles you may want to change.

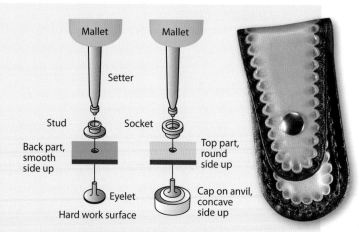

You will need:
- Awl
- Round hole punch
- Mallet
- Poly cutting board
- Flat-head screwdriver

To install:
1. Fold the belt end through the buckle, mark the hole placement with an awl, and punch round holes.
2. Insert the parts and screw in tightly.

SNAPS

These are great for handbags, clutch purses, knife pouches, small bags, belts, garments, and more.

You will need:
- Awl
- Round punch
- Rivet setter
- Anvil
- Four-part snap
- Mallet
- Poly cutting board
- Hard work surface

To install:
1. Mark the overlapping snap position with an awl.
2. Punch round holes on the marks.
3. Position snap parts as shown at right.
4. Install the stud and eyelet on the bottom part, and cap and socket on the top part using the setter, anvil, and mallet on a hard work surface. Strike the setter firmly until the parts are set.

Mallet   Mallet

Setter

Stud   Socket

Back part, smooth side up   Top part, round side up

Eyelet   Cap on anvil, concave side up

Hard work surface

SPOTS

Spots are great to use as fasteners and decoration.

You will need:

- Spots
- Craft Knife
- Ruler
- Awl or stylus
- Poly cutting board
- Mallet
- Pliers

To install:

1. Mark the spot's placement by pressing spot prongs into the leather.
2. Punch slits using an adjustable spot punch or a single thonging chisel punch (see page 32), a mallet, and a poly cutting board to protect the work surface.
3. Insert prongs in slits and bend over using pliers.

TIP: Protect spot fronts by placing them face down on a soft cloth while bending the prongs down on the back.

TIP: Plan your spot design on paper, then transfer to leather with an awl or stylus, and test on scrap leather.

TIPS FOR BELTS

These hardware pieces push onto the ends of belts, straps, etc.

You will need:

- Craft knife
- Leathercraft Cement
- Tiny screwdriver

Some tips come with tiny screws or nails on the backs.

To install:

1. Prepare the belt end by trimming or skiving just enough for the tip to slide on snugly.
2. For a secure hold, apply a small drop of cement inside the tip.
3. Some tips have tiny screws or nails on the backs for installation.

UPHOLSTERY TACKS

Use these tacks as fasteners and decoration. Decorative tacks are available with many head designs, finishes, and sizes. Patience will ensure a professional installation.

You will need:

- Upholstery tacks
- Tack hammer
- Ruler
- Awl
- Drill with a small bit

1. To evenly space tacks around a border, measure the width/diameter of the tack. Divide the length of the border to be tacked by the tack width/ diameter.
2. Mark the tack hole placement with an awl.
3. Pre-drill holes with a drill bit that's smaller than the tack shaft's diameter.
4. Tap in tacks using a tack hammer.

TIP: Use a nylon or poly head tack hammer to prevent damaging the decorative heads of the tacks.

Courtesy of Steel Strike Leather Products

ZIPPERS

Use zippers for bags, clothing, pillows, and more.

- Garment zippers can be used on most leather projects.
- If your project will have heavy wear, select a heavy-duty zipper.
- You can hand or machine stitch zippers to a leather part.
- Be sure to slick and treat the leather edges where a zipper will be installed, for a more professional look (see page 19).

GLOSSARY

Adapters: Screws that fit into the back of conchos, allowing them to be used for different purposes.

Appliqués: Separate leather pieces, tooled or plain, cemented or riveted to the surface of a leather project.

Awl: Hand tool with a sharp, pointed tip used to mark placement and to push through leather to create small holes for hand stitching and hardware installation.

Back: A side with the belly section removed. The back is firmer than the belly.

Background Dying: Technique of dying the area around a design. Normally, this area has been stamped using a background or matting tool to create a subtle or decorative pattern around the design. A fine-point brush is used.

Belly: The lower part of a side of leather. The belly has more stretch than the back.

Bend: A side of leather with the shoulder and belly trimmed off.

Bevel: Technique using a beveler stamping tool to push back leather around a cut design or border to accentuate the design or border. Also refers to rounding the cut edge of a piece of leather using an edge beveler hand tool.

Block Dying: A coloring technique using a wooden block wrapped in cotton cloth. Dye is applied to the block that is stroked over a tooled surface, leaving dye on just the high points of the design.

Bone Folder: Originally made of bone, now bone or plastic, used to fold, crease leather, and slick and burnish edges.

Buckle Prong: The tongue part on a buckle that pushes through the holes on a belt or strap.

Burnishing: When the top grain of veg-tanned leather is compressed or stamped, the area darkens or burnishes.

Calfskin: Leather made from skins of young cattle.

Casing: Dampening veg-tan leather with water in preparation for tooling.

Chisels: Punches used with mallet or maul to punch slits for lacing or stitching.

Chrome Tanned: Process of tanning leather using chromium compounds. This tanning process produces soft leathers used in garments, upholstery, and footwear.

Combination Tanned: Tannage of two or more agents, such as chrome and vegetable.

Creaser: Hand tool used to impress fold and border edge lines in leather.

Crocking: Transferring color or finish from leather to other material by rubbing or by abrasion.

Drive Punch: Tool used with a mallet or maul to punch holes in leather.

Dyeing: Coloring technique using water-based or alcohol-based colors manufactured specifically for leather usage.

Embossing: The technique of pressing a manufactured die into cased leather. Also means raising areas of a design by pressing up from the back side of cased leather using modeling tools or fingers.

Eyelet: A metallic protective hardware ring that inserts into a hole, then is set with a special setter that flares the inside edge to secure it in place, protecting and strengthening the hole.

Filigree: Technique of cutting out the intricate background around and inside of a tooled design.

Finishing: Applying a protective leather coating over natural or dyed leather to help seal the surface from moisture and protect it from wear.

Flesh Side of Leather: The underside of leather.

Forming: Technique of molding or embossing dampened leather into different shapes.

Full Grain or Top Grain: Terms used to describe the outer surface or grain side of skin from which the hair has been removed.

Gouging: Using hand tools to cut into the top grain of leather, leaving a trench for design or hand stitching, or on the back for a fold.

Grain Side: The top, smooth, outer side of a piece of leather that the hair grew out of.

Hair-on: Hides and skins that have hair still on the grain side.

Hide: The whole pelt of a large animal.

Inverted Carving: Technique of tooling a design in reverse, meaning instead of tooling the background into the leather allowing the design to be on the surface, inverted carving pushes the design into the leather, allowing the area around it to be on the surface, framing the design.

Kidskin: Skin of a young goat.

Leather: The hide or skin of an animal or any portion of the skin, which has been prepared or tanned for use.

Latigo: Cattle hide leather tanned and used for outdoor wear, saddler work, and military accoutrements.

Mallet: A hammer with poly, rawhide, or wooden heads used in leatherwork, in order not to harm the tools. Metal hammers will damage stamping tools and punches. Mallets come in a variety of sizes and weights.

Maul: A type of mallet with a vertical striking surface normally made with a poly head used in leatherwork. Mauls come in a variety of sizes and weights.

Modeler: A hand tool, normally with two different ends, used to scribe, form, and burnish leather. Also used during lacing to help pull stitches tight and even.

Molding: Technique of forming dampened leather into different shapes.

Ounce (oz.): Term used to indicate thickness of leathers. Historically, one square foot of leather weighs a certain number of ounces and will uniformly be of a certain thickness. An ounce of leather is equivalent to 1/64 (.0156) inch in thickness.

Punching: Using a rotary punch or single drive punches with a mallet on a cutting board to cut holes or shapes into leather.

Rawhide: This is the American name for hide that has been dehaired and limed, sometimes oiled or gone through other processes, but has not been tanned.

Reenactment: The re-staging of historical events, authentically or not, with costuming, accouterments, and appropriate landscaping and animals.

Resists: Technique used in coloring leather that uses different finishes to prevent dyes and stains from penetrating the leather, creating different hues and effects.

Rivet: Hardware, plain or decorative, used to join leather or to decorate projects. A special setter is used along with a mallet or maul.

Setters: Handy tools used to assemble hardware components.

Shoulder–Single: Left or right side part of the hide between the neck and the main body of the hide.

Shoulder–Double: Both the left and right side parts of the hide between the neck and the main body of the hide.

Side: Half of a hide or skin of leather.

Skin: The whole pelt of a small animal.

Skive: The technique of shaving leather with a sharp knife or skiving tool, to make it thin and less bulky.

Slicker: A hand tool used to form, slick, and burnish edges of leather.

Splicing: In lacing, splicing is when you join two pieces of lace together at their ends.

Staining: A coloring technique using semitransparent dyes.

Stamps: Hand tools, either with a separate design head with a handle or an all-in-one tool to be tapped into cased veg-tan leather using a mallet or maul on a hard surface.

Stropping: Polishing a knife blade using a firm surface and rouge. Helps keep a blade edge sharp.

Suede: Leather that has been sanded or buffed to create a nap. It denotes a finish, not a type of leather.

Swivel Knife: "The" leather carver's tool. Called "swivel" because the yoke is designed to turn while using, to allow the carver to easily make curved cuts in leather. Available in many different styles and sizes with different detachable blades.

Tanning: Chemical and mechanical processes used to convert the animal skins or hides into a stable product that is no longer susceptible to rotting.

Tracing: Copying a design or pattern from a drawn or printed piece onto tracing paper or vellum using a pen or pencil.

Transfer: The procedure to convey a traced pattern from tracing paper or vellum onto cased leather using a stylus, pen, or pencil.

Veg-Tanned: A generic term to cover the process of making leather using tannins from barks, woods, or other part of plants and trees, along with chemicals. The process used to produce tooling leather.

Vellum: Semitransparant, water-resistant tracing paper used for transferring designs.

Weight: Term used when measuring the thickness of leather.

Wing Divider (Compass): A drafting and leatherworking tool used to scribe a guideline along a straight or curved edge, or to scribe a circle.

ACKNOWLEDGMENTS

We wish to thank:

Silver Creek Leather Company
Greg Sartor and Kristi Hauptstueck, for supporting us during the creation of this book. Tom Brown, for sharing his leather knowledge. Sara Anderson, for proofing. Jessica Miller, for help with photography.

Steel Strike Custom Leather Products, Buena Vista, CO
Philip Smith, owner and president, for allowing us to show samples of your beautiful, custom, leather-accented furniture and accessories.

Leather Crafters & Saddlers Journal
Charil Reis and Ralph Solome, for allowing us to use our project Journal photos and for years of supporting the leather craft industry with shows and teaching venues. www.leathercraftersjournal.com

Fox Chapel
Thank you for publishing our book and making it available to all leather crafters.

INDEX